CHORD SUBSTITUTIONS

A chord substitution, as the words imply, simply means replacing or inserting chords to create harmony that is more interesting and oftentimes more challenging to the player. In this book the substitutions or reharmonizations are indicated in red. The black chord symbols beneath them essentially represent the original harmony.

First of all, there are really only two types of chord substitutions:

- Replacing existing chords
- Inserting a chord or chords between existing chords.

In both cases, the object is to enhance (color) the process of getting from point A to point B, that is, the original harmonic progression. In fact, the function of harmony in general is to get from point A to point B and then return to point A. This can be seen in the following example which is harmonic progression in its most basic form:

The obvious next and most simple step in adding interest to this progression is the addition of the Subdominant chord — inserted between the Tonic and the Dominant. This has become the harmonic foundation of popular music.

Let's take the song "Merrily We Roll Along" as an example of this. Notice that the song would be fine with just the C and G7 chords. However, the addition (insertion) of the IV (Subdominant) chord gives the harmony a bit more color.

This will serve as our framework as we begin to further explore possibilities of chord substitutions. But first, let's discuss the importance of root movement.

ROOT MOVEMENT

The root of a chord is determined by the letter name of the chord symbol. For example, the root of Cmaj9 is C. How the roots of chords move from one to another is an important tool in understanding the concept of chord substitutions.

Here are some important root movements:

- **Cyclical** (by 4ths or 5ths)

Examples: D7 → G7 → C7
Em7 → A7 → Dmaj7

• **Chromatic** (by 1/2 steps)

Examples: Am7 → A♭dim → Gm7
Gmaj7 → G♯dim → Am7 → A♯dim → Bm7

• **Diatonic** (by scale steps)

Examples: C → Dm7 → Em7
Dmaj7 → C♯dim7 → Bm7 → Amaj7

• **Tritone** (A leap of three whole steps with a downward resolution of 1/2 step)

Examples: Gm7 → D♭13 → C7
F7 → B7♭9 → B♭maj9

RELATING ROOT MOVEMENT TO CHORD SUBSTITUTIONS

Now, let's use these various root movements to explore their relationship to chord substitution.

The cyclical movement of roots is the most common and is one that is extremely strong. One chord is pulled toward the next almost like harmonic gravity. Here is an example of adding **cyclical** root movement to "Merrily We Roll Along:"

The letters I and R that appear above the substitutions refer to the type of substitution used: Insertion or Replacement.

Notice that by adding the chord substitutions we have a better and more interesting way to get from point A to point B (C → G7; and G7 → C).

Now here's the same tune but with **chromatic** root movement as a method of chord substitution:

Again, in this example, it is important to recognize how strongly the chords pull to one another as well as the new colors that are brought to the progression.

Here is an example of using stepwise, **diatonic** root movement to create new harmonic colors:

Finally, here is an example from our harmonic palette of **tritone** root movement which resolves downward by 1/2 step:

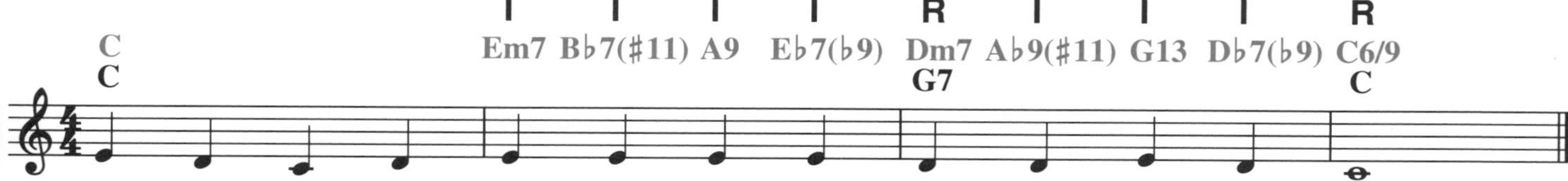

Note: This is a reharmonization of our cyclical example.

This exercise might seem a bit excessive or redundant. However, it clearly demonstrates that the opportunities to utilize this type of substitution are abundant.

DIAGONAL SLASHES—SLASH CHORDS

Diagonal slashes are used in this book when the bass note (right of the slash) is not the same as the root of the chord symbol (left of the slash). These slash chords appear frequently throughout this book and represent an important part of the chord substitution process.

It should be noted that the roots of the chords and the bass notes of slash chords do not necessarily dictate the bass line to be played (note for note). They do, however, represent the contour of the overall bass line and reinforce the importance of linear motion:

Here is an example:

Special Note:

As you play and experiment with the various types of chord substitutions, you'll see more and more of the logic behind this exciting musical technique. In this case and many others...**LEARNING IS THE PERCEPTION OF PATTERNS.**

AULD LANG SYNE

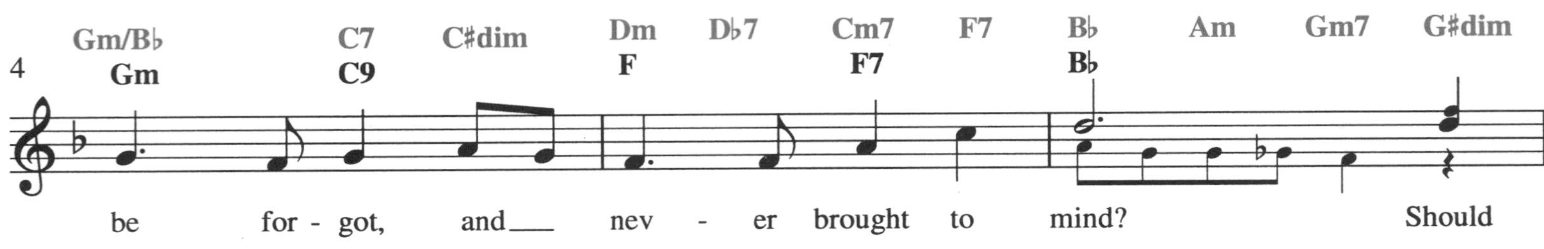

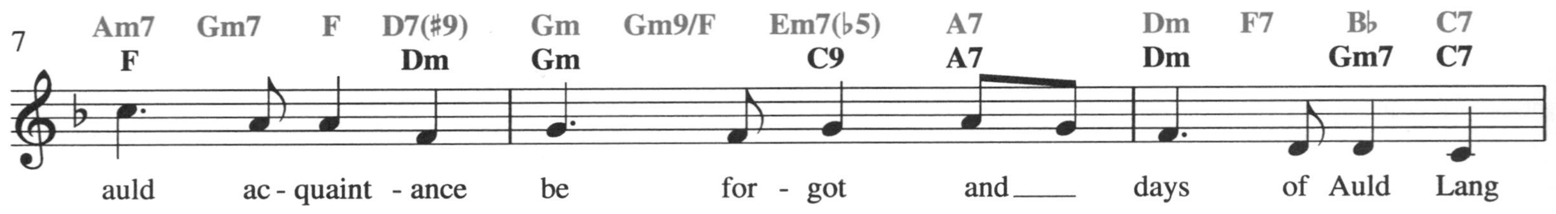

For a swing arrangement of this song, try doubling the time values, so that each measure (from above) becomes two. For example:

AWAY IN A MANGER

Words and Music by
MUELLER

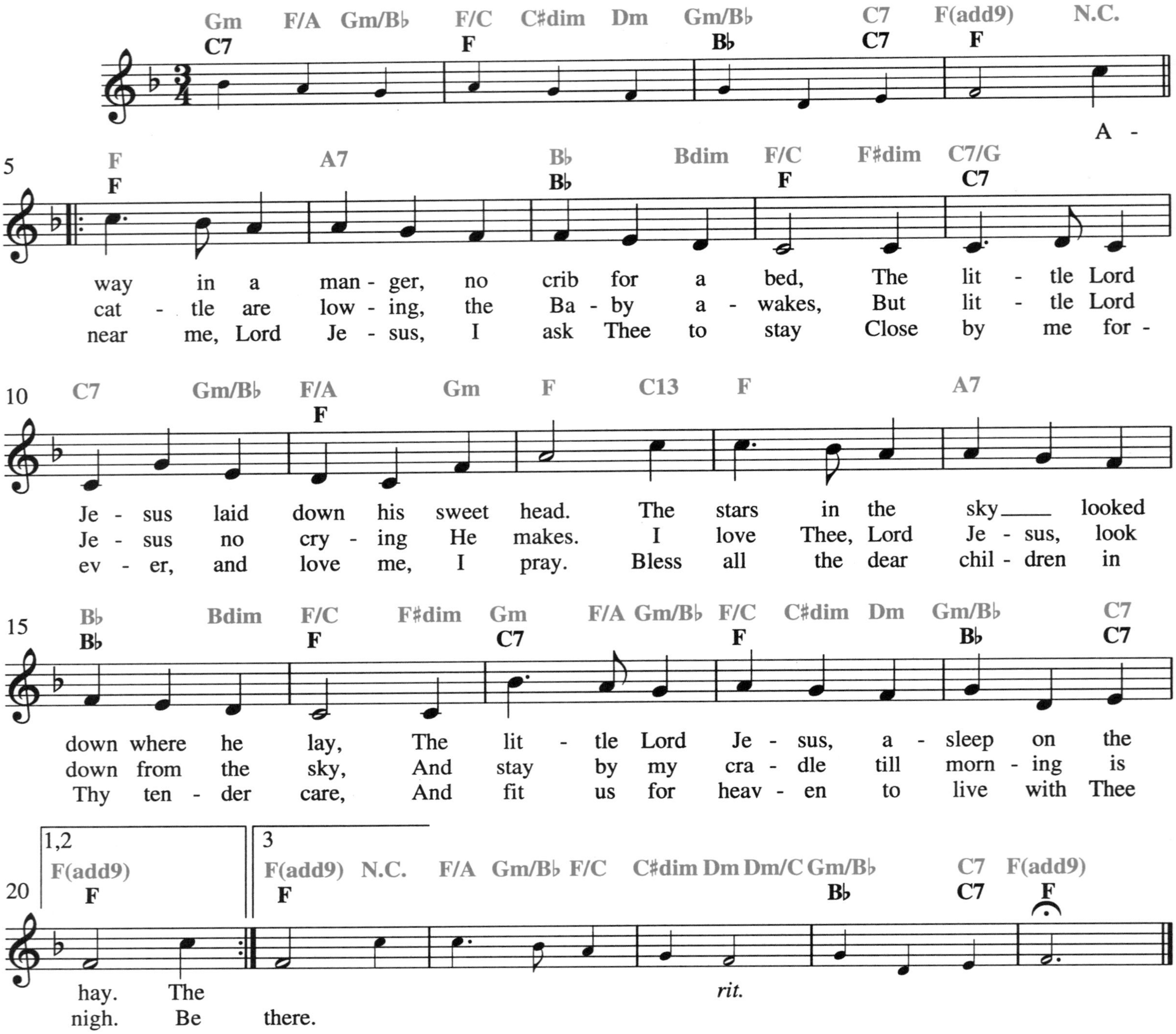
Gm F/A Gm/B♭ F/C C♯dim Dm Gm/B♭ C7 F(add9) N.C.
C7 F B♭ C7 F
A -
F A7 B♭ Bdim F/C F♯dim C7/G
F B♭ F C7
way in a man - ger, no crib for a bed, The lit - tle Lord
cat - tle are low - ing, the Ba - by a - wakes, But lit - tle Lord
near me, Lord Je - sus, I ask Thee to stay Close by me for -
C7 Gm/B♭ F/A Gm F C13 F A7
F
Je - sus laid down his sweet head. The stars in the sky looked
Je - sus no cry - ing He makes. I love Thee, Lord Je - sus, look
ev - er, and love me, I pray. Bless all the dear chil - dren in
B♭ Bdim F/C F♯dim Gm F/A Gm/B♭ F/C C♯dim Dm Gm/B♭ C7
B♭ F C7 F B♭ C7
down where he lay, The lit - tle Lord Je - sus, a - sleep on the
down from the sky, And stay by my cra - dle till morn - ing is
Thy ten - der care, And fit us for heav - en to live with Thee
1,2
F(add9)
F
3
F(add9) N.C. F/A Gm/B♭ F/C C♯dim Dm Dm/C Gm/B♭ C7 F(add9)
F B♭ C7 F
hay. The
nigh. Be there.
rit.

1. Notice the effectiveness of the contrary motion caused by the bass line of the substitutions, (most obvious in bars 17-19). Throughout, the bass line is moving in a direction opposite to that of the melodic contour. This reinforces the tension and release of each phrase.

2. Here is an example of a simple arpeggio for an F(add9) chord.

F(add9)
etc...
Play an octave lower

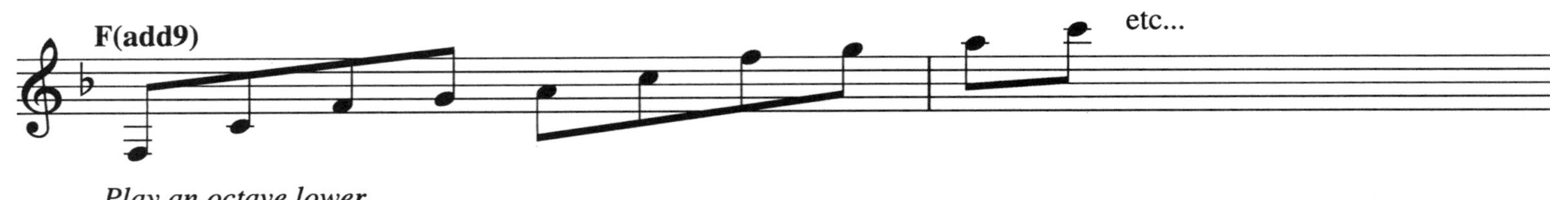

BECAUSE IT'S CHRISTMAS
(For All The Children)

Words and Music by BARRY MANILOW, BRUCE SUSSMAN & JACK FELDMAN

C E7(#5) Fmaj9 Dm7 Bb7 G7/B
C(add9) C Fmaj7 F6 Dm Gsus G
C C E7(#5) F Dm7
C C(add9) C Fmaj7 F6
To-night the stars shine for the chil - dren.
To-night be - longs to all the chil - dren.
Bb7 G7/B C E7 Am C#dim
Dm Gsus G C Am Am(maj7) Am7
and light the way for dreams to fly. To-night our love comes wrapped in
To-night their joy rings through the air. And so, we send our ten - der
Dm Dm/C Bb7 G7/B C Em/B
Dm7 F/G G7 C
rib - bons. The world is right and hopes are high.
bless - ings to all the chil - dren ev - 'ry - where.
Am Am/G F#m7(b5) F7
Am G/F F
And from a dark and frost - ed win - dow a child ap -
To see the smiles and hear the laugh - ter; a time to
E7sus E7 Am Am/G 1 F6 Dm7
E7sus E7 Am Dm7
pears to search the sky be - cause it's Christ - mas, be - cause it's
give, a time to share be - cause it's

2
18
G9 G7/B
F/G G
Christ - mas.
Fm7 A♭/B♭
A♭
Christ - mas for now and for - ev - er
C/G
C/G
for all of the
21
Am7 D7
Am7 C/D D
chil - dren and for the
F/G Em/G Dm/G G7
F/G G7
chil - dren in us
C E7(♯5)
C
all.
24
F6 Fm6
Fmaj7 F6
A♭/B♭
A♭/B♭
Cm/B♭ B♭ A♭/B♭ B♭7
Cm/B♭ B♭ A♭/B♭ B♭
27
E♭ G7(♯5)
E♭
To - night be - longs to all the
A♭ Fm7
A♭maj7 A♭6
chil - dren.
29
D♭7 B♭7/D
Fm7 Fm7/B♭ B♭7
To - night their joy rings through the
E♭ G7/D
E♭(add9) E♭
air.
31
Cm Edim
Cm Cm(maj7) Cm7
And so, we send our ten - der
Fm Fm/E♭
Fm7
bless - ings
33
D♭7 B♭7/D
A♭/B♭ B♭
to all the chil - dren ev - 'ry -
E♭ Gm/D
E♭
where.

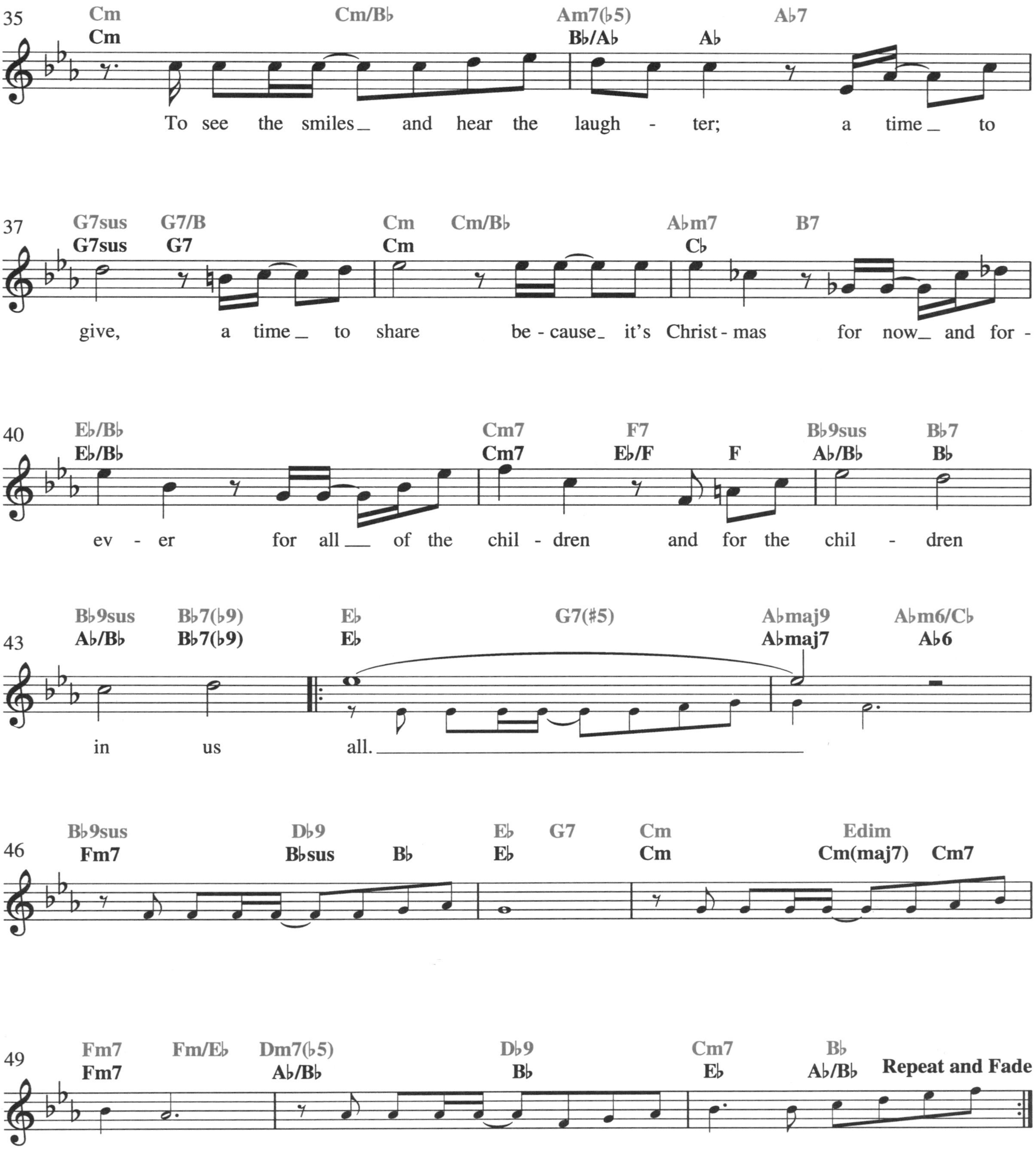

35 Cm Cm/B♭ Am7(♭5) A♭7

Cm B♭/A♭ A♭

To see the smiles_ and hear the laugh - ter; a time_ to

37 G7sus G7/B Cm Cm/B♭ A♭m7 B7

G7sus G7 Cm C♭

give, a time_ to share be - cause_ it's Christ - mas for now_ and for -

40 E♭/B♭ Cm7 F7 B♭9sus B♭7

E♭/B♭ Cm7 E♭/F F A♭/B♭ B♭

ev - er for all_ of the chil - dren and for the chil - dren

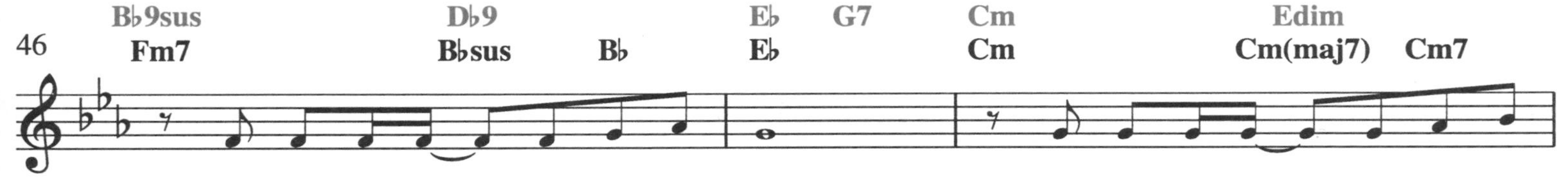

BLUE CHRISTMAS

Words and Music by BILLY HAYES
and JAY JOHNSON

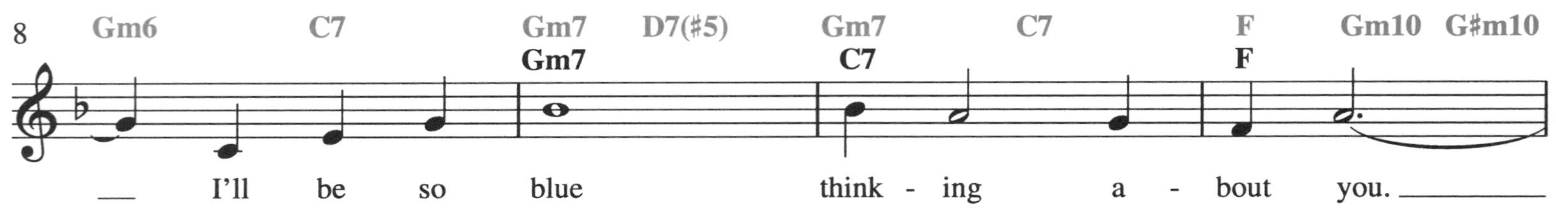

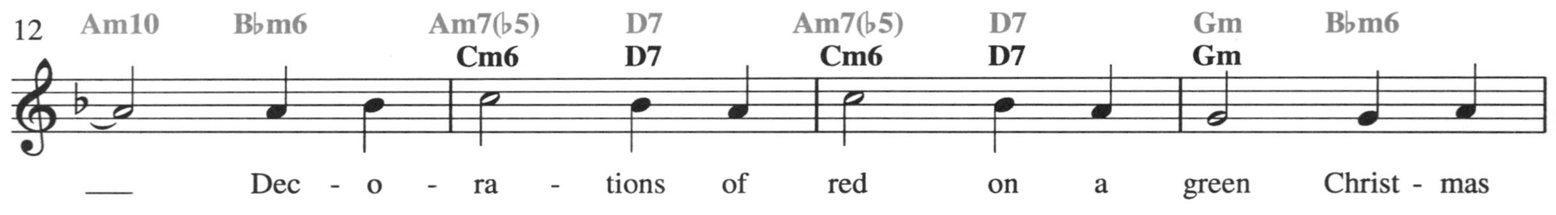

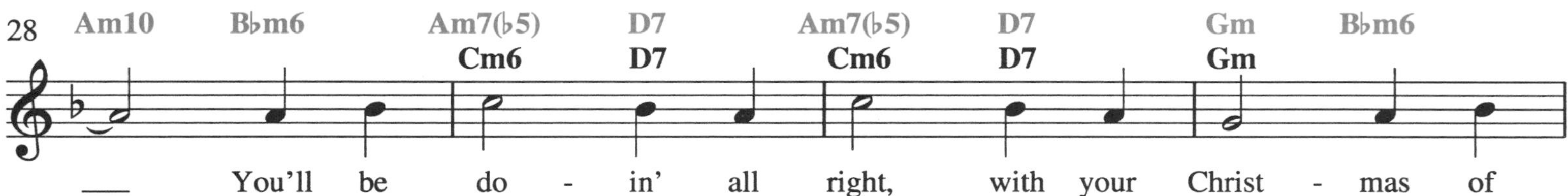

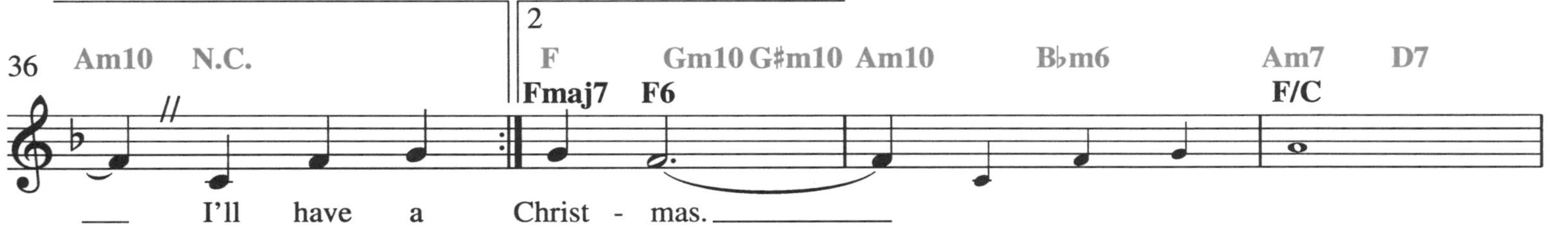

A chord symbol followed by the number 10 indicates that the root and 3rd of the chord are to be played at the interval of a tenth, and the fifth is to be omitted. To do this, simply move the 3rd up one octave. This voicing usually appears in a succesion of chords, as seen in this example:

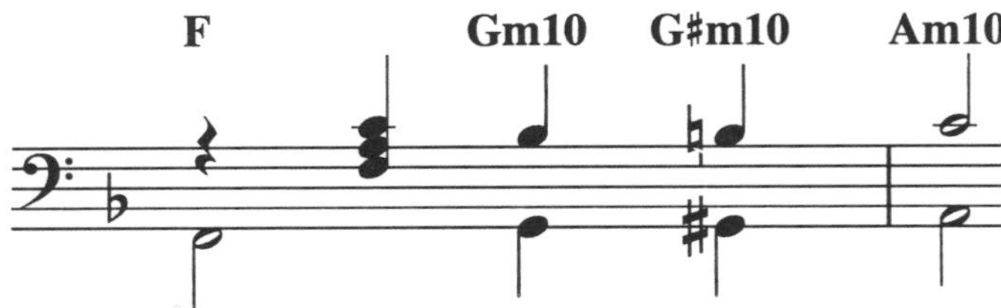

This type of progression is generally used to embellish an otherwise static harmony (since the original, in this case, stays on an F chord).

THE CHIPMUNK SONG

Words and Music by
ROSS BAGDASARIAN

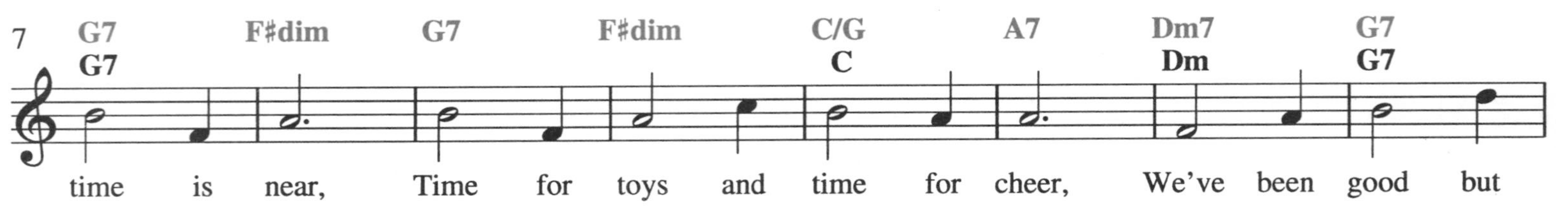

As an alternative to the F#dim which is used frequently, try playing a Dm7 instead. It might be best to mix it up a bit, that is, leave some F#dim chords in place while replacing others selectively.

DECK THE HALL

Additional Lyrics

2. See the blazing Yule before us, Fa la la la la, la la la la.
Strike the harp and join the chorus, Fa la la la la, la la la la.
Follow me in merry measure, Fa la la, la la la, la la la.
While I tell of Yuletide treasure, Fa la la la la, la la la la.

3. Fast away the old year passes, Fa la la la la, la la la la.
Hail the new, ye lads and lasses, Fa la la la la, la la la la.
Sing we joyous all together, Fa la la, la la la, la la la.
Heedless of the wind and weather, Fa la la la la, la la la la.

CHRISTMAS IS

Lyrics by SPENCE MAXWELL
Music by PERCY FAITH

Eb Cm7 Fm7 Bb9
Eb Cm7 Fm7 Bb7
Christ - mas is sleigh bells, Christ - mas is shar - ing,
3
Eb Cm7 Fm7 Bb9 Eb Cm7
Eb Cm7 Fm7 Bb7 Eb6 Cm7
Christ-mas is hol - ly, Christ-mas is car - ing. Christ-mas is child - ren who
Christ-mas is car - ols to
6
Fm7 Bb13 Eb Cm7 Fm7 Bb7 Em7 A7
Fm7 Bb9 Eb6 Cm7 Fm7 Bb9 Eb9 Eb7
just can't go to sleep. Christ-mas is mem-'ries, the kind you al - ways keep.
warm you in the snow. Christ-mas is bed - time where no one wants to go.
9
Ab6 Adim Bb7 G7/B Cm7 Dm7(b5) G7/B
Ab6 Fm7 Bb9 Eb6 Cm7 Fm7 G7(#5)
Deck the halls and give a cheer for all the things that Christ-mas is each
All the world is tin - sel bright, So glad to know that Christ-mas is to
12
Cm Cm/Bb Am7(b5) Abm6 Eb/G C7(b9)
Cm Ab6 Abm Abm6 Eb
year. Christ - mas, mer - ry Christ - mas, when
night. Christ - mas, mer - ry Christ - mas, when
15
1
Fm7 Bb9 Eb Edim Fm9 Bb13
Fm7 Bb7 Eb6 Abmaj7 Bb13
all your wish - es come true.
2
Fm7 Bb9 Eb Db9(#11) C9
Fm7 Bb7 Eb Db7(b5) C7
all your wish - es come true.

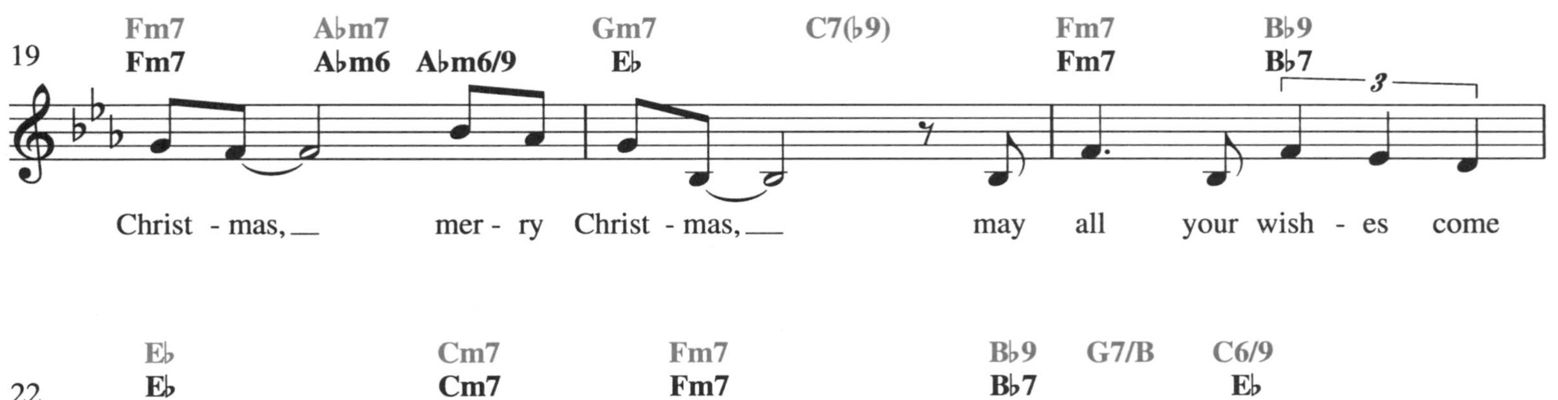

When creating chord substitutions (and in general harmonic practice) it is important to select target chords to which the progressions lead. Quite frequently, the target chord is the tonic (I) chord. In this case, however, it is the Cm7 of bar 10 (VIm7). Notice the chromatic motion of the bass line, starting on the A♭6 of bar 9. Substituting the E♭6 with the G7/B (secondary dominant in inversion) in bar 10 makes the target chord (Cm7) even stronger.

CHRISTMAS IS A-COMIN'
(May God Bless You)

Words and Music by
FRANK LUTHER

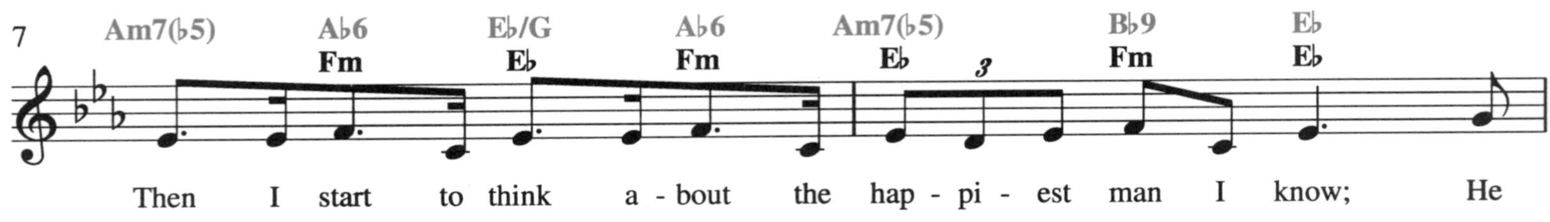

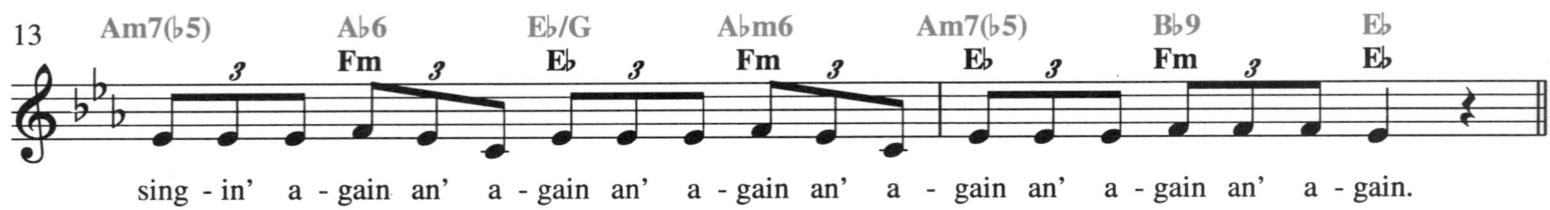

The melody of this song is wistful, with a touch of sadness, even though it is in a major key. This sentiment is reflected in the substitutions in bars 6-8, and again in bars 10-14.

THE CHRISTMAS SONG

(Chestnuts Roasting On An Open Fire)

Music and Lyric by MEL TORME
& ROBERT WELLS

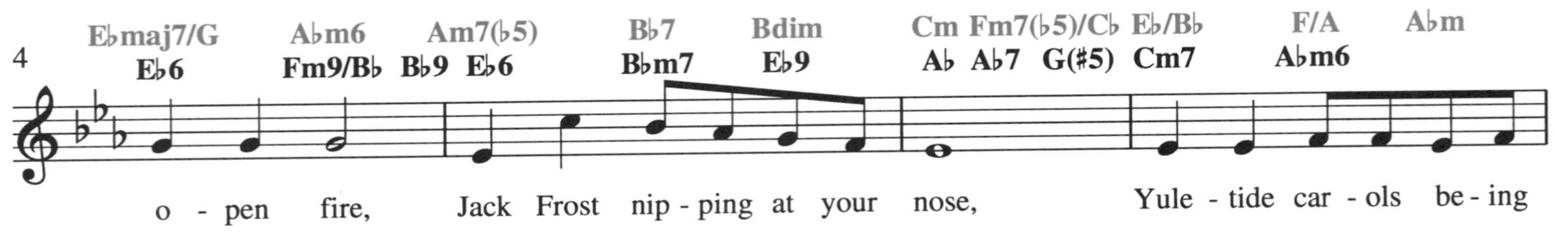

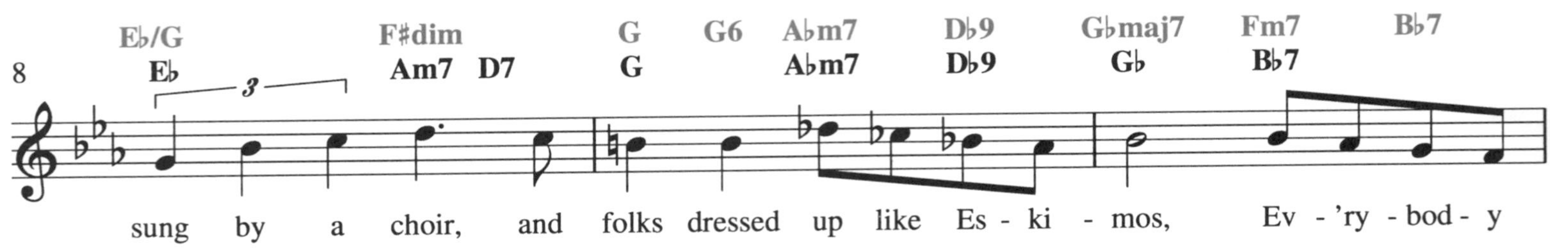

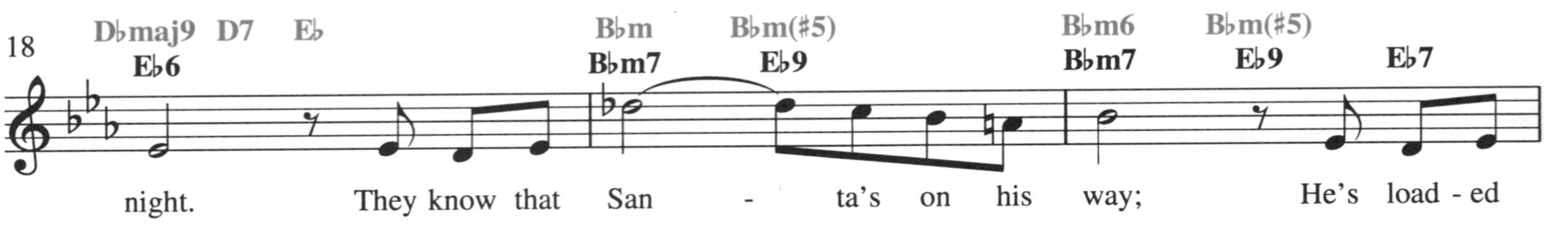

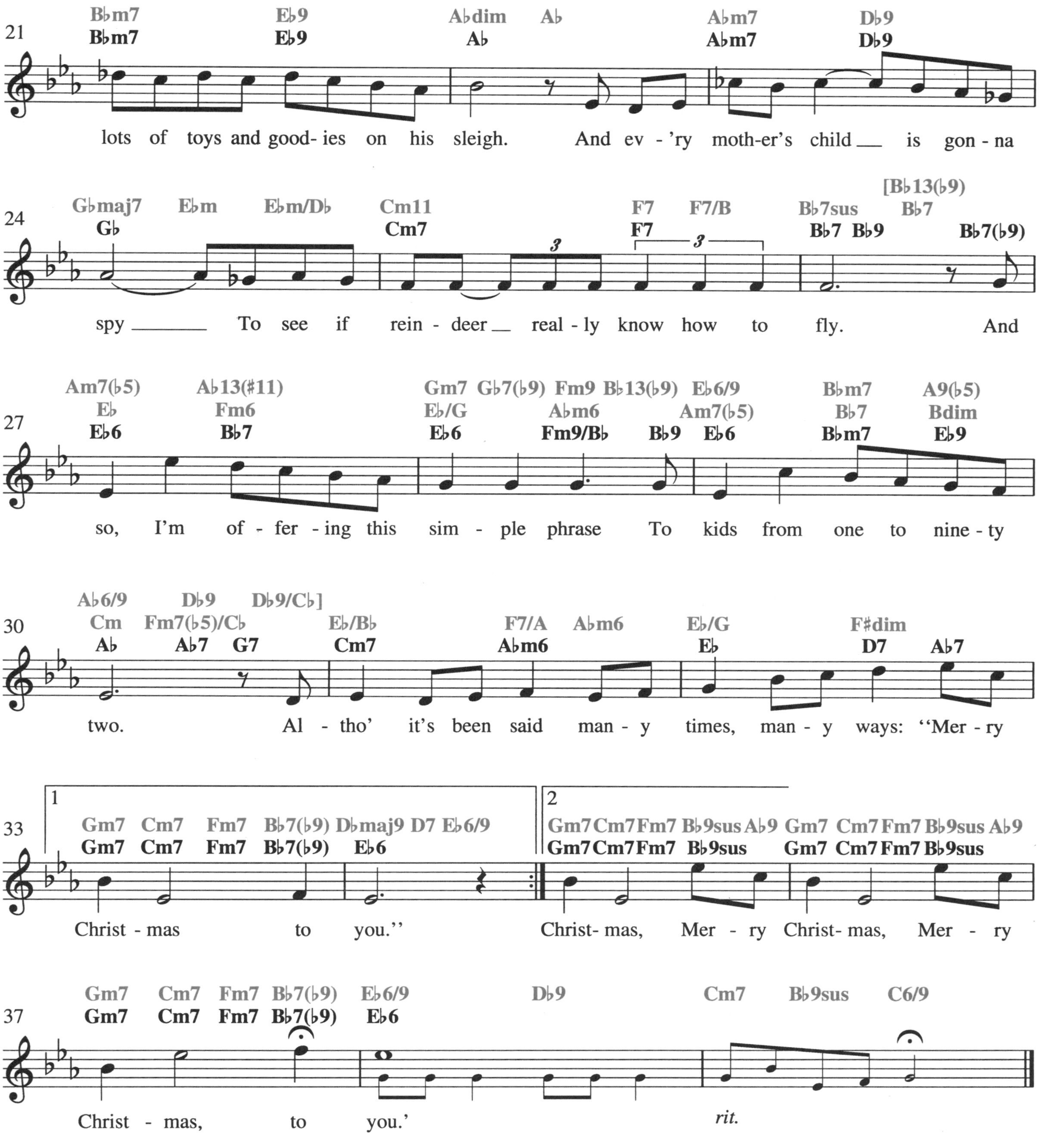
21
B♭m7 E♭9 A♭dim A♭ A♭m7 D♭9
B♭m7 E♭9 A♭ A♭m7 D♭9
lots of toys and good- ies on his sleigh. And ev - 'ry moth-er's child is gon - na
24
G♭maj7 E♭m E♭m/D♭ Cm11 F7 F7/B B♭7sus [B♭13(♭9) B♭7
G♭ Cm7 F7 B♭7 B♭9 B♭7(♭9)
spy To see if rein - deer real - ly know how to fly. And
27
Am7(♭5) A♭13(♯11) Gm7 G♭7(♭9) Fm9 B♭13(♭9) E♭6/9 B♭m7 A9(♭5)
E♭ Fm6 E♭/G A♭m6 Am7(♭5) B♭7 Bdim
E♭6 B♭7 E♭6 Fm9/B♭ B♭9 E♭6 B♭m7 E♭9
so, I'm of - fer - ing this sim - ple phrase To kids from one to nine - ty
30
A♭6/9 D♭9 D♭9/C♭]
Cm Fm7(♭5)/C♭ E♭/B♭ F7/A A♭m6 E♭/G F♯dim
A♭ A♭7 G7 Cm7 A♭m6 E♭ D7 A♭7
two. Al - tho' it's been said man - y times, man - y ways: "Mer - ry
33
1
Gm7 Cm7 Fm7 B♭7(♭9) D♭maj9 D7 E♭6/9
Gm7 Cm7 Fm7 B♭7(♭9) E♭6
Christ - mas to you."
2
Gm7 Cm7 Fm7 B♭9sus A♭9 Gm7 Cm7 Fm7 B♭9sus A♭9
Gm7 Cm7 Fm7 B♭9sus Gm7 Cm7 Fm7 B♭9sus
Christ- mas, Mer - ry Christ- mas, Mer - ry
37
Gm7 Cm7 Fm7 B♭7(♭9) E♭6/9 D♭9 Cm7 B♭9sus C6/9
Gm7 Cm7 Fm7 B♭7(♭9) E♭6
Christ - mas, to you.'
rit.

In bars 19-26, the substitute chords suggest a chromatic counter melody:

40
B♭m B♭m(♯5) B♭m6 B♭m(♯5) B♭m7 E♭9 A♭dim A♭
etc...

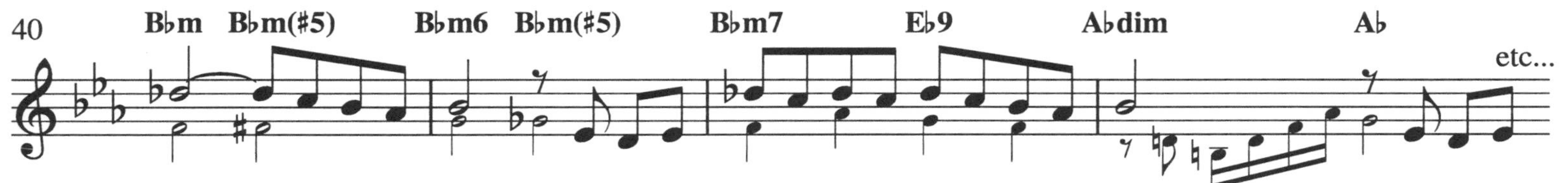

THE CHRISTMAS WALTZ

Words by SAMMY CAHN
Music by JULE STYNE

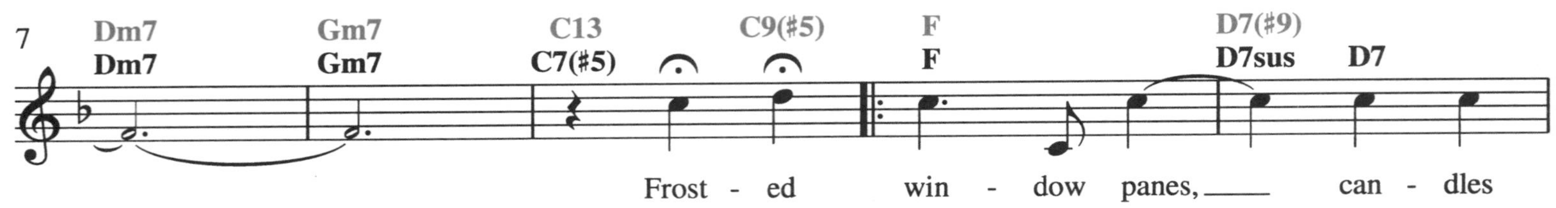

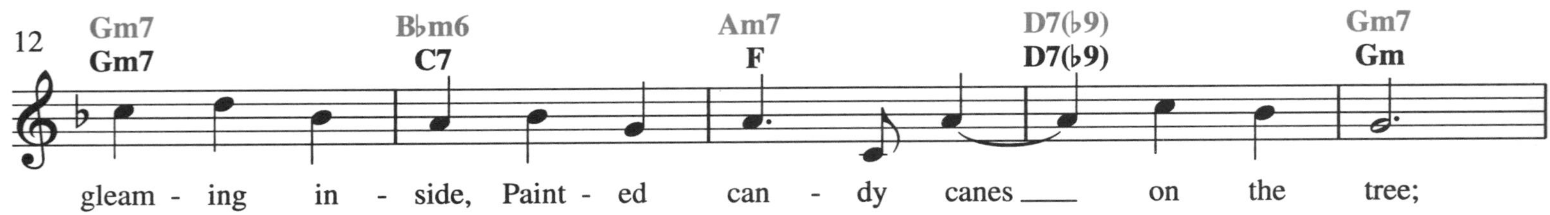

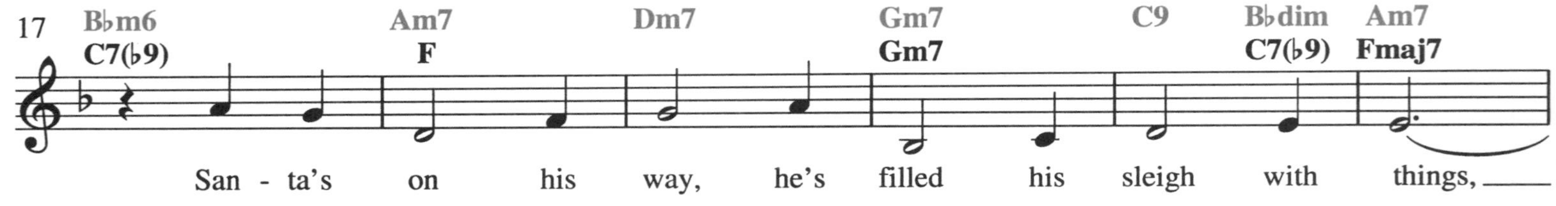

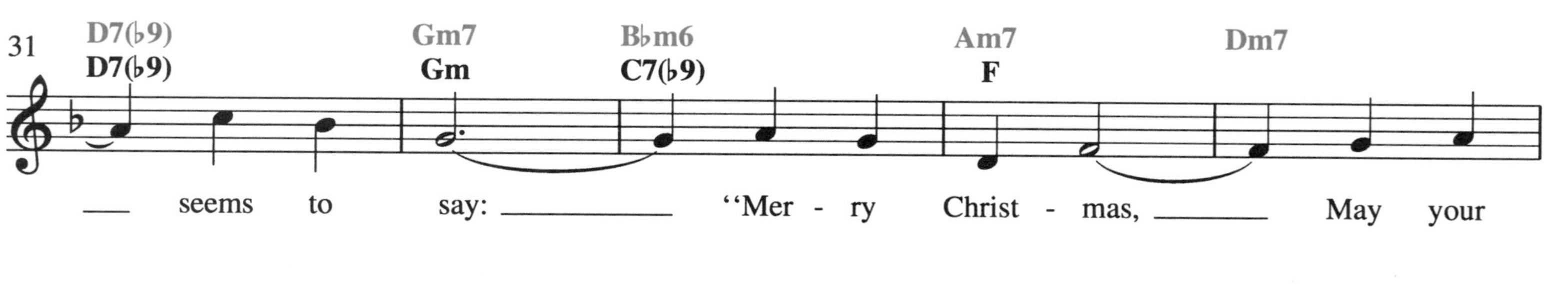

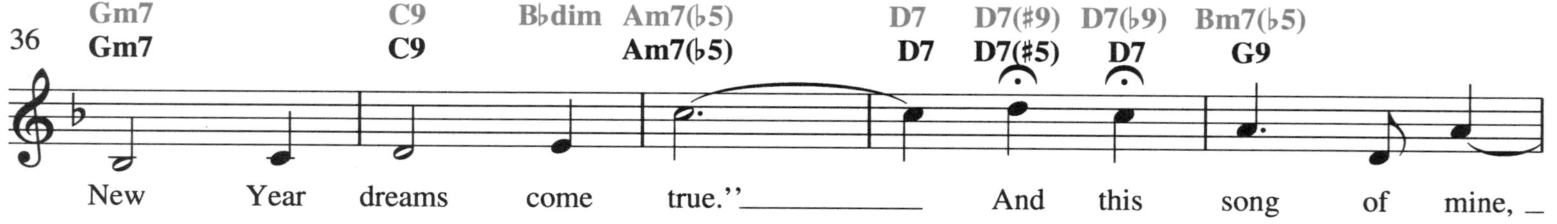

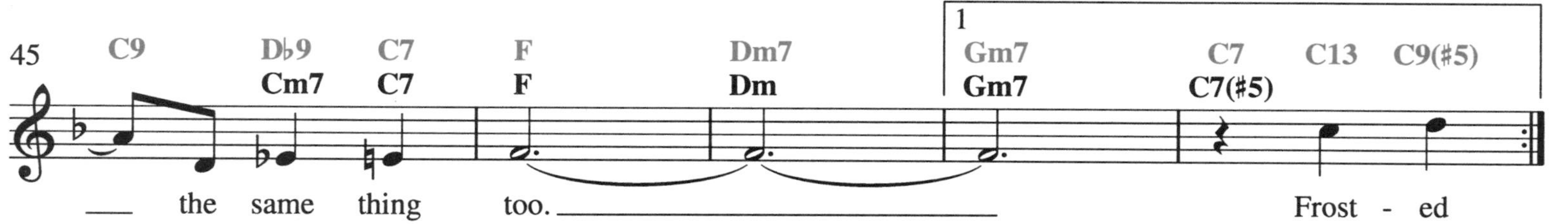

The measures of $\frac{2}{4}$ in the Intro and Ending should be played freely. Therefore, the waltz tempo doesn't begin until bar 6. Here is a suggested way of voicing the top line of chords in both the Intro and Ending:

THE FIRST NOEL

THE GREATEST GIFT OF ALL

Words and Music by
JOHN JARVIS

25 C/E G7/D C G7/D C/E Am7 D7 D7/C
C G Am D7
air. All the gifts are wait - ing for chil-dren ev - 'ry -
29 G/B F/A G7 C G7/D C/E Fmaj7 F#m7(♭5) F7
G F G C G C C7 F
where. Through the win - dow I can see snow be - gin to
33 C/E Am Dm7 G7 F6 C/E F C/E F G7
C G C F C G
fall. Know-ing you're in love with me is the great - est gift of
37 C C/B♭ A7 A10 Bm10 C#m10 D A7/E D/F# Gmaj7
C A7 G A7 D A D
all. Just be-fore I go to sleep
41 E7/G# Em/G D/F# A7/E D A7/E D/F# Gmaj7
G D A Bm Bm7
I hear a church bell ring. Mer-ry Christ - mas ev - 'ry - one
45 E/G# G A7 G/B A7/C# D A7/E D/F# Gmaj7
E7 A G A7 D A D
is the song it sings. So I say a si - lent prayer
49 E/G# G D/F# Bm Em7 A7 D7 G
G D A7 D7 G
for crea-tures great and small. Peace on earth good will to men is the

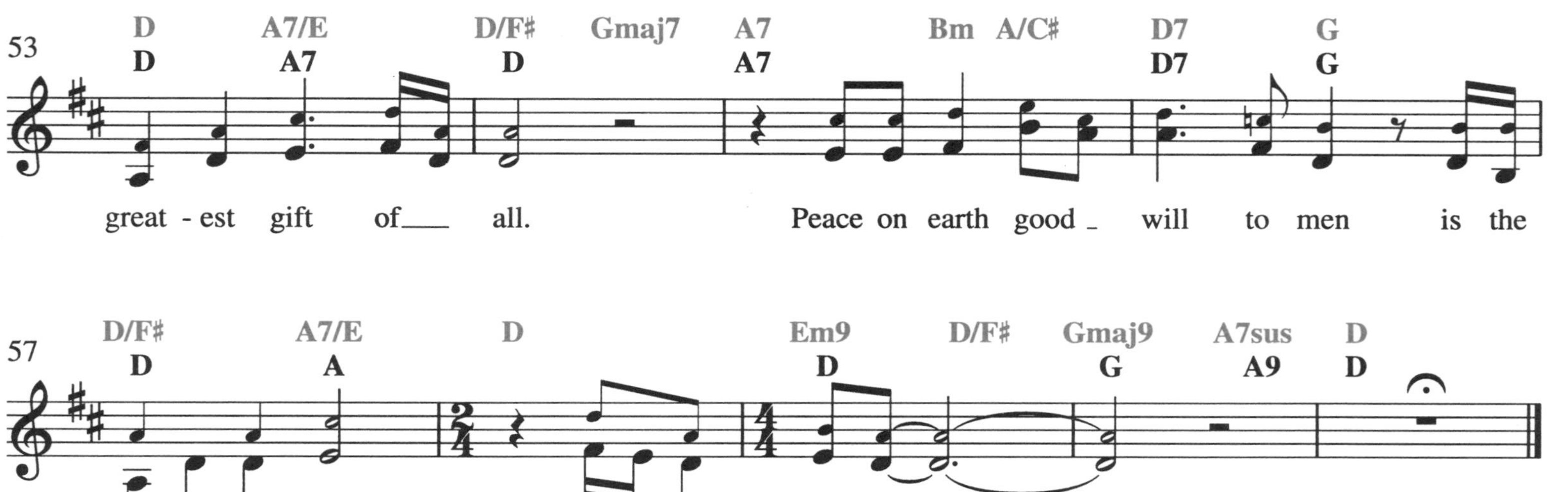

Here is a suggested accompaniment for piano using the substitute chords:

FROSTY THE SNOW MAN

Words and Music by STEVE NELSON
and JACK ROLLINS

28
C C#dim G/D Em7/B F9 E9 Am7 D7 G G7/B
C G Ddim Am7 D7 G G7
found. For when they placed it on his head he be - gan to dance a - round. Oh,
cop. And he on - ly paused a mo - ment when he heard him hol - ler, ''Stop!'' For

33
C C/B C/A C7/G G♭7 F F#dim C/G G♭7
C C7 F C
Fros - ty the snow man was a - live as he could be, And the
Fros - ty the snow man had to hur - ry on his way, But he

37
F F#dim C/G A7 Dm7 G7 C
F C Am A7 Dm7 G7 C
chil - dren say he could laugh and play just the same as you and me.
waved good - bye say - in' ''Don't you cry, I'll be back a - gain some day.''

41
Cmaj9 C6 C7(♭9) Cmaj9 C#dim Dm7 G7
C G7
Thump-et - y thump thump, thump-et - y thump thump. Look at Fros - ty go.

45
C#dim G7/D Cm6/E♭ G7/D G7 G#dim Am6 G7/B C
C
Thump-et - y thump thump, thump-et - y thump thump. O - ver the hills of snow.

HAPPY CHRISTMAS, LITTLE FRIEND

Lyrics by OSCAR HAMMERSTEIN II
Music by RICHARD RODGERS

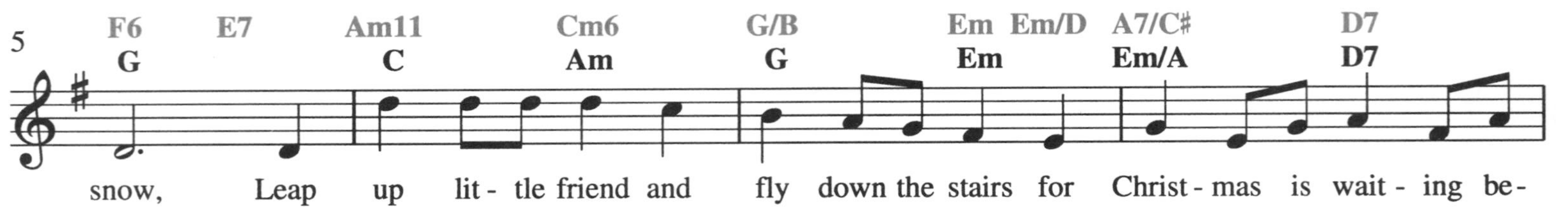

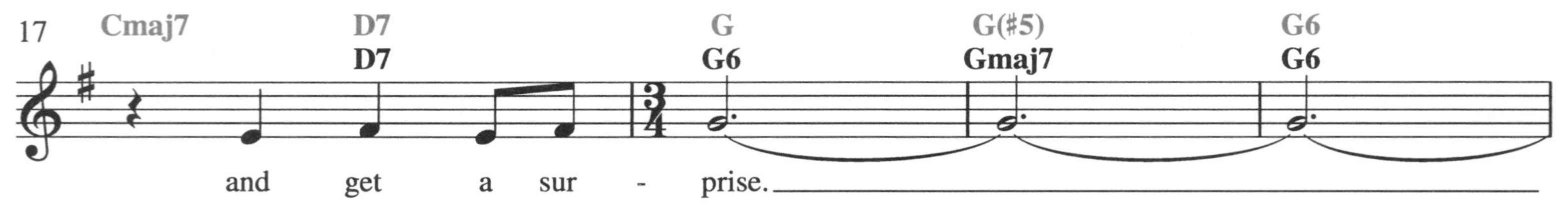

25
Gm/B♭ Am7 D9 C9 G/B
Em/D Am D7 Em6
friend, May your heart be laugh - ing all day.
29
Gm/B♭ Am7 D9 C9 Bm7
G Am Am/D G
May your joy be a dream you'll re - mem - ber,
33
Em7 Am7 D9 G G(♯5)
Am D7 G6
As the years roll a - long on their way.
37
G6 G♯dim Am7 D9 C9 Bm7
Am D7 Gmaj7
As the years roll a - long on their way
41
E7(♭9) Am7 D9 C9 Bm7
G6 Am D7 Gsus2/B
you'll be show - ing your own kid a tree.
45
E7(♯9) E7(♭9) Am7 D9 C9 G/B
G/B Am D7 G6
Then at last, my friend, you'll
49
Gm/B♭ Am7 D9 C9 F9(♯11)
Am D7 G7/D
know How hap - py a Christ - mas can be,

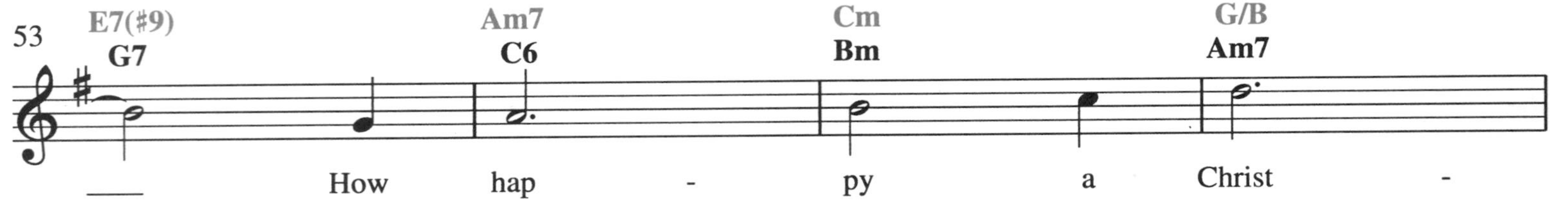

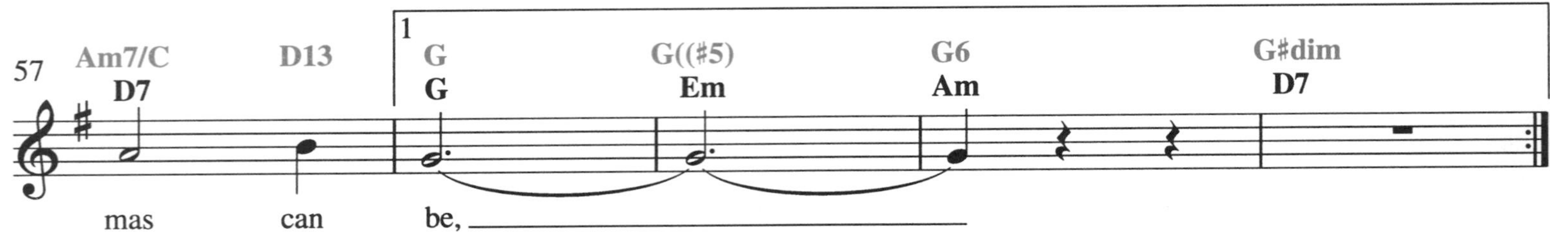

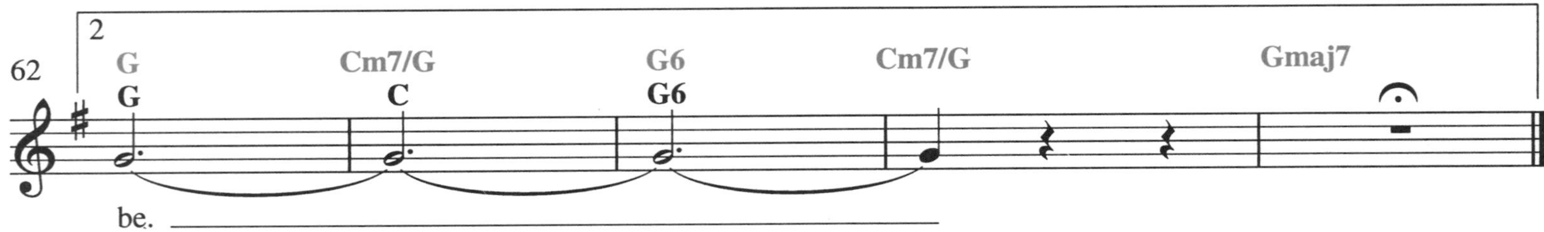

1. The first 17 bars (in 4/4) can be played out of time, following the vocalist (or instrumentalist). ''Time'' then begins at bar 18 where the meter changes to 3/4.
2. In the second ending, the substitute Cm7/G chords are a bit of a surprise. When playing a fill over the ending, it would be advisable to emphasize the E♭ and B♭ of the Cm7 chord.

HAPPY XMAS (WAR IS OVER)

Words and Music by JOHN LENNON
and YOKO ONO

14
A A/C# G/D B/D# Em G
A G F#m Em G
To Coda
Year, let's hope it's a good one ___ with - out an - y
16
D/F# E E7 A C#m7 D6 A/C#
D E E7 A Amaj7 D6 A
fear. And so this is X - mas for weak and for
(War is o - ver
18
Bm F#7/C# Dmaj7 E7 Bm7 E7 Bm E13
Bm Bm(maj7) Bm9 Bm E7sus E7 Bm7 E7
strong The rich and the poor ones the road is so ___
if you want it war is o - ver
20
A E/G# D/F# A/E Bm A G D/F#
A E7 Bm A D Dmaj7 G6
long. And so, Hap - py X - mas for black and for
now.) ___ (War is o - ver
22
Em D#dim Em9 A7 D A/C# Em/B A13
Em Em(maj7) Em9 Em A7sus A7 Em7 A7
white, For the yel - low and red ones let's stop all the
if you want it war is o - ver
24
D F#m G D13 G Em7
D A7 Em D13 G
fights. ___ A mer - ry, mer-ry X - mas ___ And a hap - py New
now) ___

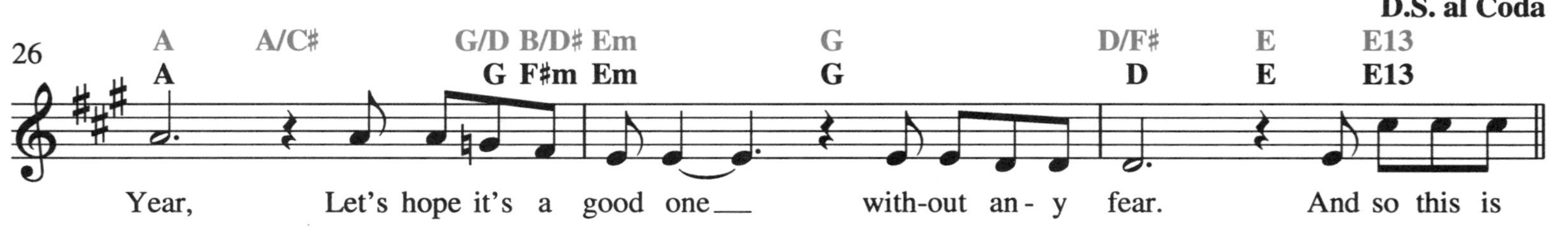

The counter-melody which begins in bar 5 comes directly from the chords.

HAPPY HANUKKAH, MY FRIEND

(The Hanukkah Song)

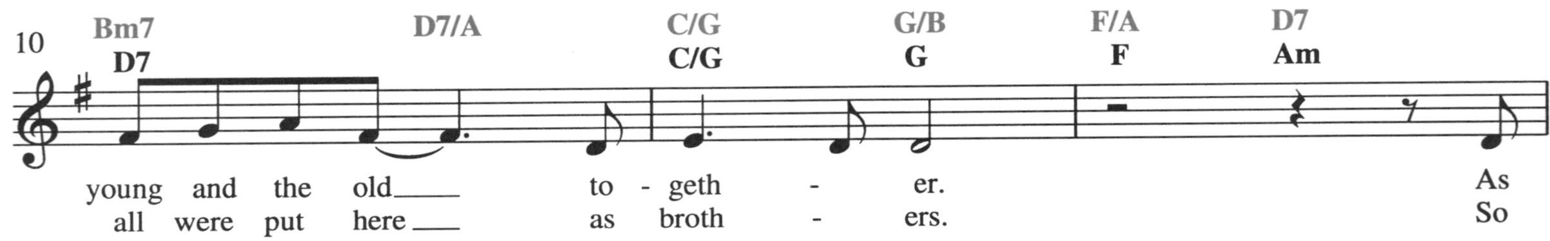

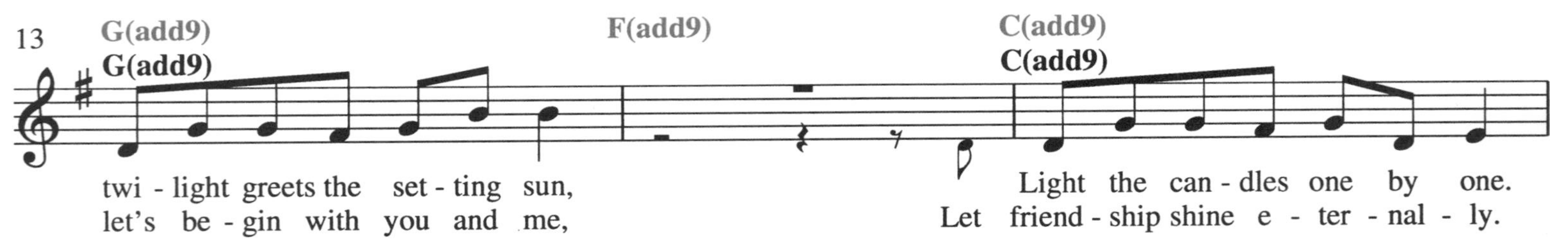

19
C/G G/B C D7sus G G6
C/G G C/D G
ev - er.
oth - ers.
Come, let's
22
F9 F♯m7(♭5) B7 Am7 D7
Em7 Am G D
share the joy of Ha - nuk - kah. May our
25
Am Am/G F♯m7(♭5) B7(♯5) Em Cm/E♭
F♯m7(♭5) B7 Em
friend - ship grow, as the can - dles glow.
28
D C D G G6 F9
D G Em7
Oh, won't you come and share the joy of
31
F♯m7(♭5) B7 F♯m7(♭5) F9 Em C/E
Am G F♯m7(♭5) B7 Em
Ha - nuk - kah;
And we'll cel - e - brate as
And we're hop - ing all you're
34
Em6 Em7 C♯m7(♭5)
Em/D A(add9)/C♯
on - ly friends, can do.
wish - ing for comes true.
37
G/D Cmaj7/D
G/D C/D
1
G(add9)
G(add9)
Hap - py Ha - nuk - kah, my friend, from me to you.

40
F(add9)
C(add9)
Em7sus
F(add9)
D7sus
Am7(add4)

43
2
G
G
Cmaj7/D
C/D
G
G
Hap - py Ha- nuk - kah, my friend,

46
C/D
C/D
G(add9)
G(add9)
F(add9)
from me to you.

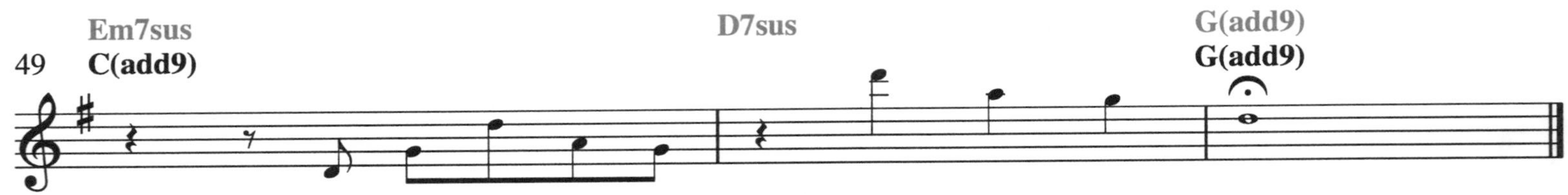

49
Em7sus
C(add9)
D7sus
G(add9)
G(add9)

HAPPY HOLIDAY

Words and Music by
IRVING BERLIN

This tune invites transposition. On beat 3 of bar 20 just play the dominant chord of whatever key you wish to enter, then proceed to transpose the melody and chords to suit the new key.

HARD CANDY CHRISTMAS

Words and Music by
CAROL HALL

1. The Bass line indicated in the introduction can be used over the same chords in the verse at bars 5-8 and 13-16. Note that it returns in the Coda.
2. The introduction can be played as a ''vamp til ready'' intro by repeating the E♭maj9 and A♭maj9 until someone cues the verse.

A HOLLY JOLLY CHRISTMAS

Music and Lyrics by
JOHNNY MARKS

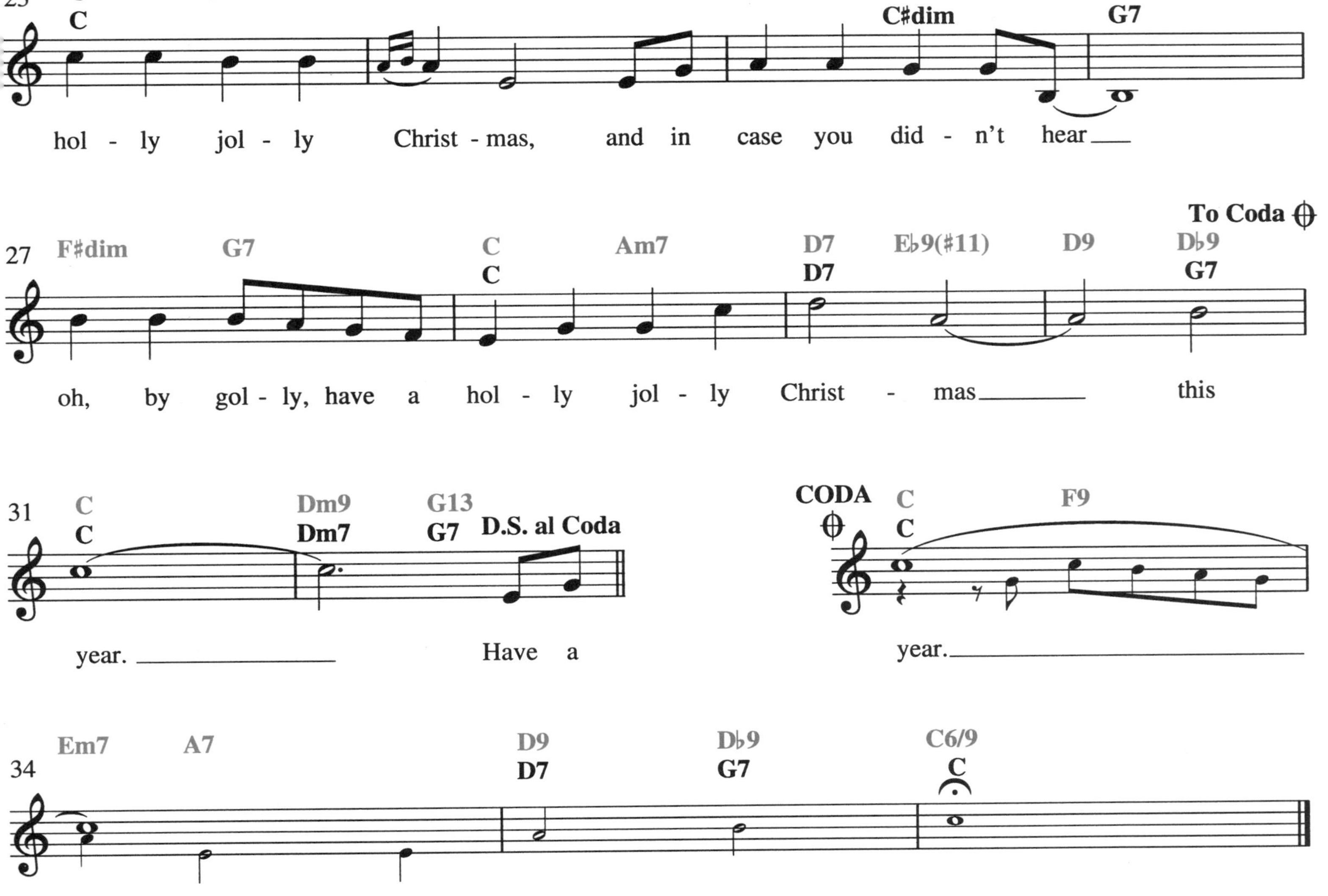

When creating intros and endings, it helps make the arrangement coherent if the material is related to the song. In this case, notice how the melody of the first two bars of the refrain (bars 5-6) is manipulated two different ways to ''drive'' the ideas for the intro and ending.

(There's No Place Like)

HOME FOR THE HOLIDAYS

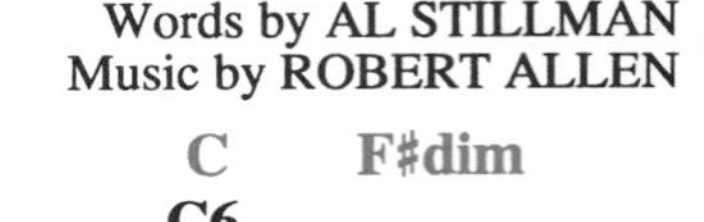

Words by AL STILLMAN
Music by ROBERT ALLEN

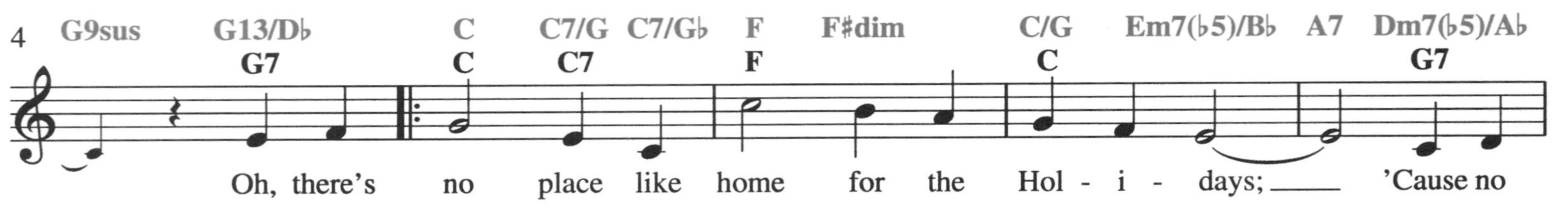

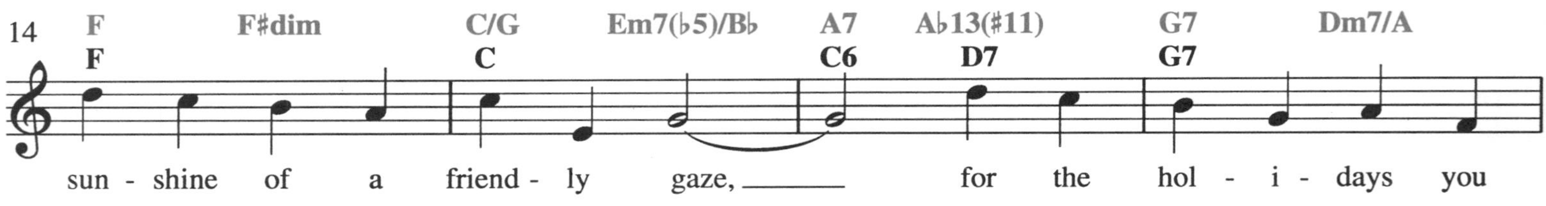

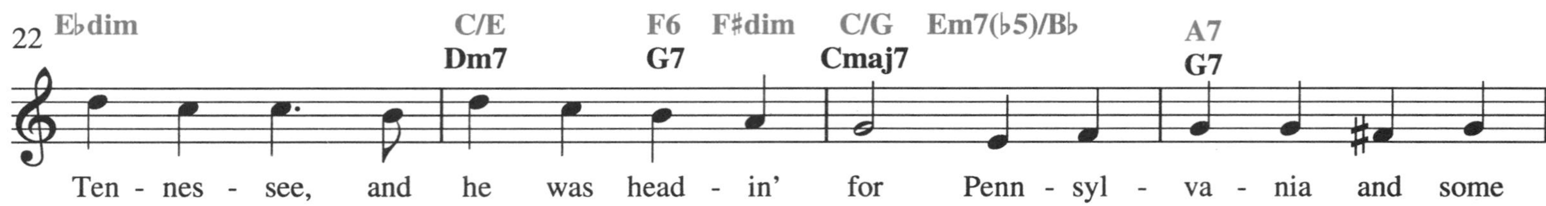

26
D13 G7 C Dm10 E♭m10 Em10 F6 A7/E Dm
Dm7 G7 C6 F
home - made pump - kin pie. From Penn - syl - va - nia folks are
30
E♭dim C/E F6 F♯dim C/G C♯dim G/D E7
Dm7 G7 Cmaj7 G
trav - 'lin' down to Dix - ie's sun - ny shores; From At - lan - tic to Pa -
34
Am7 D13 G7 C♯dim Dm7 G13 C C7/G C7/G♭
Am7 D7 G7 C♯dim Dm7 G7 C7
cif - ic, gee, the traf - fic is ter - rif - ic. Oh, there's no place like
38
F F♯dim C/G Em7(♭5)/B♭ A7 Dm(♭5)/A♭ C/G B9 B♭9
F C G7 C
Home for the Hol - i - days 'cause no mat - ter how
42
A9 Bm7(♭5) Dm/C C♯m7(♭5) D7 D7/A♭ G9sus G13/D♭ C C7/G C7/G♭ F F♯dim
Dm7 Em F6 F♯dim G7sus G7 C7 F
far a - way you roam, If you want to be hap - py in a
47
C/G Em7(♭5)/B♭ A7 A♭13(♯11) G7 Dm7/A
C D7 G7
1
B♭dim G7/B C Dm10 E♭m10
Dm7 G7 C6
mil - lion ways For the hol - i - days you can't beat home, sweet home.
52
Em10 Fmaj7 G7
G7
2
B♭dim C♯dim Dm7 G9 C
Dm7 G7 C6
Oh, there's can't beat home, sweet home.

I HEARD THE BELLS ON CHRISTMAS DAY

Words by HENRY LONGFELLOW
Adapted by JOHHNY MARKS
Music by JOHNNY MARKS

N.C.
N.C.
I
5
F F/A Gm/B♭ Am Gm7 F E7 Am7 D7
F F(♯5) B♭ C7 Dm Dm6 F E7 Am
heard the bells on Christ - mas day, their old fa - mil - iar car - ols play: And
in des-pair, I bowed my head, "There is no Peace on Earth," I said, "For
9
Gm7 C7 C/B♭ Am7(♭5) D7 Gm7 B♭m6 Bm7(♭5) C7
Gm C7 Am7(♭5) D7 Gm D7 Dm6 C7
wild and sweet the words re - peat, Of Peace On Earth Good Will To Men. I
Hate is strong and mocks the song Of Peace On Earth Good Will To Men." Then
13
F A7 B♭ G/B C C/B♭ F/A B♭ F/A E7/G♯ Am7 D7
F F(♯5) B♭ C7 Dm Dm6 F E7 Am
thought, as now this day had come, The bel - fries of all Chris - ten - dom Had
pealed the bells more loud and deep, "God is not dead, nor doth He sleep. The
17
Gm7 C7 C/B♭ Am7(♭5) D7
Gm C7 Am7(♭5) D7
1
Gm7 B♭m6 G/B C7 F N.C.
Gm D7 Dm6 Gm7 C7 F C7
rung so long the un - bro - ken song Of Peace On Earth, Good Will To Men. And
wrong shall fail, The right pre - vail, With
2
21
Gm7 B♭m6 G/B C7sus F N.C. F6/9
Gm D7 Dm6 Gm7 C7 F N.C.
Peace On Earth, Good Will To Men."

IT CAME UPON THE MIDNIGHT CLEAR

I SAW MOMMY KISSING SANTA CLAUS

Words and Music by
TOMMIE CONNOR

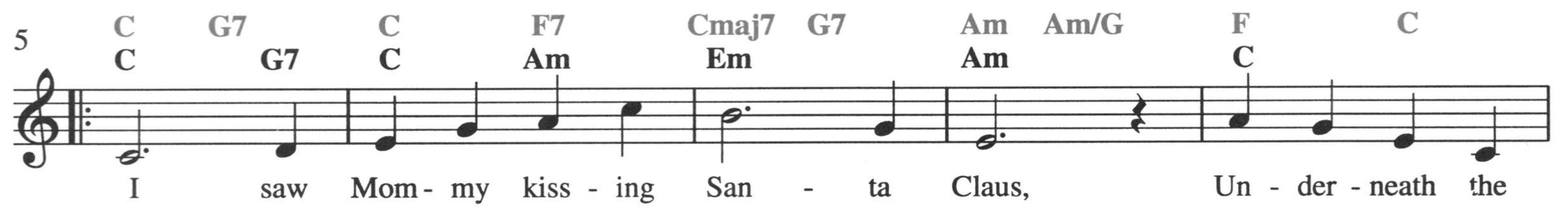

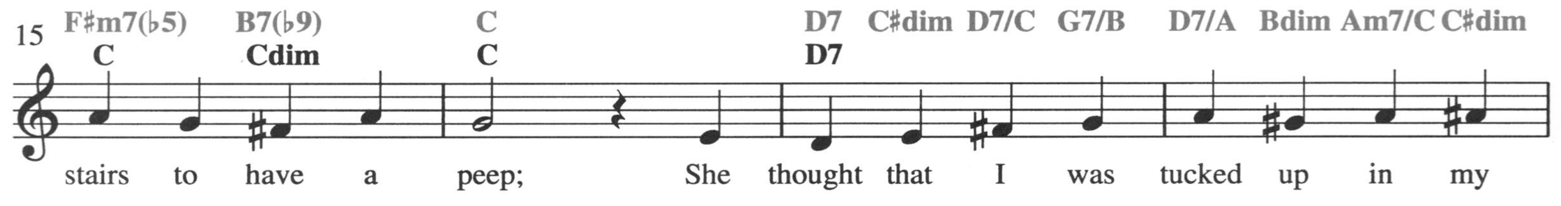

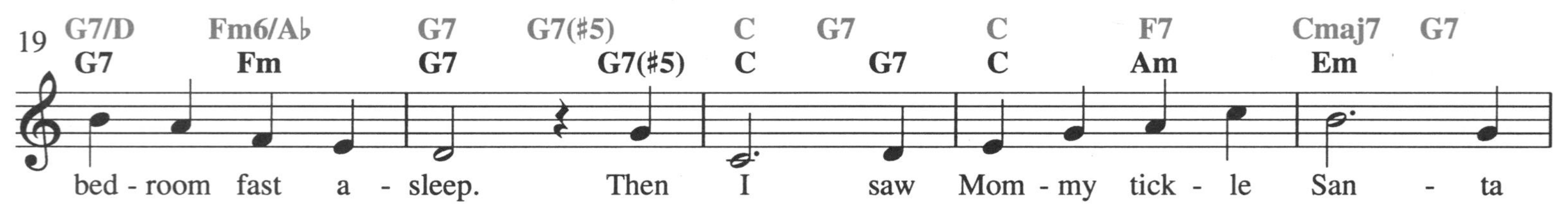

28
Dm
Dm
F
F
F♯dim
B7
C/G
C
A7
A7
Oh, what a laugh it would have been, If Dad - dy had on - ly
32
Dm7
Fm6/A♭
Dm7
G7
C/G
C
Am7
F
A♭13
Fm
G9
G7
1
C
E♭dim
Dm7
G7(♯5)
C E♭dim Dm7 G7
seen Mom - my kiss - ing San - ta Claus last night.
2
37
C
Slowly
E7/B
Am7
D7
A♭13
G13
F9
Cmaj7
C
Dm7
C6
Cmaj7
C
night.

I STILL BELIEVE IN SANTA CLAUS

Words and Music by MAURICE STARR
and AL LANCOLLOTTI

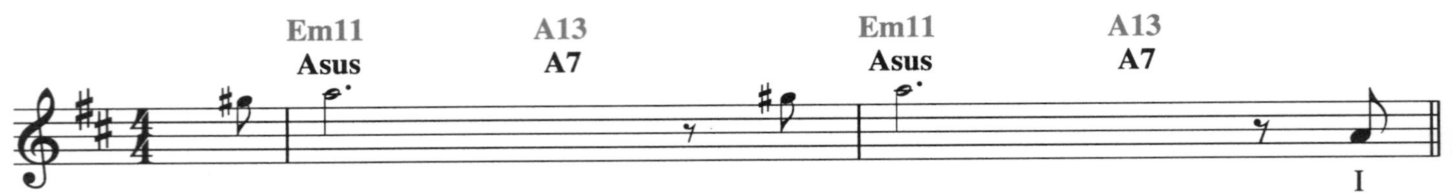

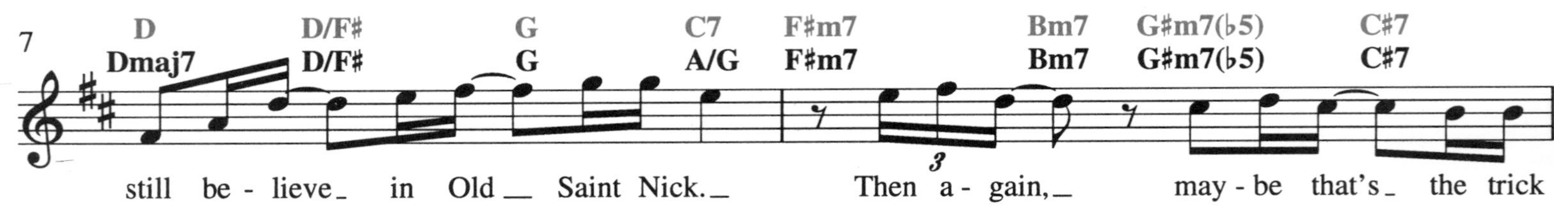

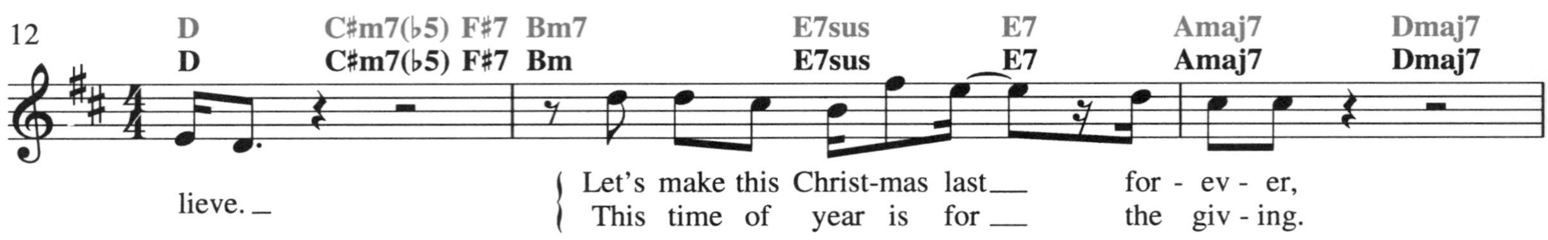

15
Gmaj7 F9 Em11 A7 Dmaj9 E♭7(♯9)
G Em7 A7 Dmaj7
shine in love a - long the way. For the
This time of year is for the joy. May
17
Dm9 G13 Cmaj7 E7/B Em11 A13
Dm7 G7 E7sus E7 A7sus A7
sake of all the chil - dren let love show us the way.
joy and hap - pi - ness be with you al - ways this day.
20
1
Em11 A13
A7sus A7
I
2
Em11 A13
A7sus A7
D.S. al Coda
I
CODA
Em7 A7
Em7 A
world of make be -
23
D C7 Bm7 Gm/B♭ D6/A D7/A♭
D A/D G6/D Gm6/D D
lieve, from a world of make be - lieve.

I'LL BE HOME FOR CHRISTMAS

Words and Music by KIM GANNON
and WALTER KENT

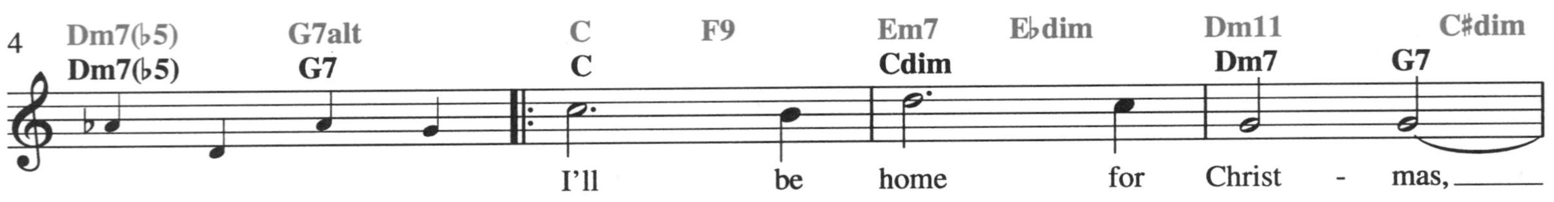

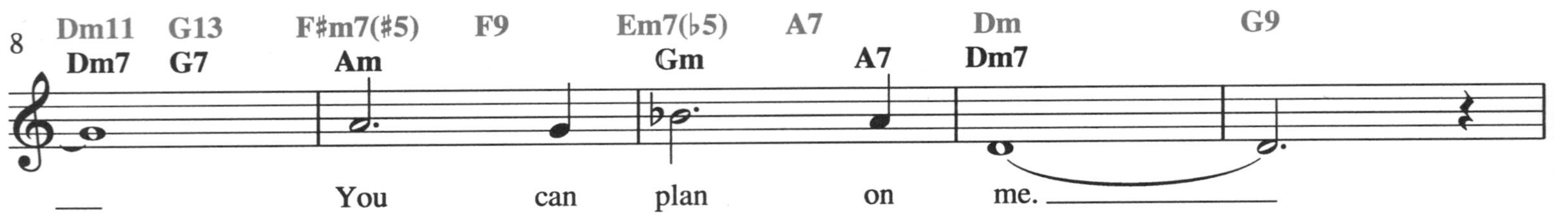

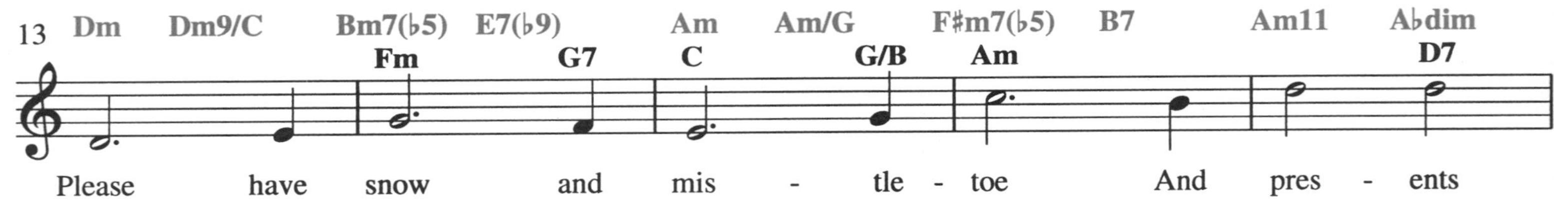

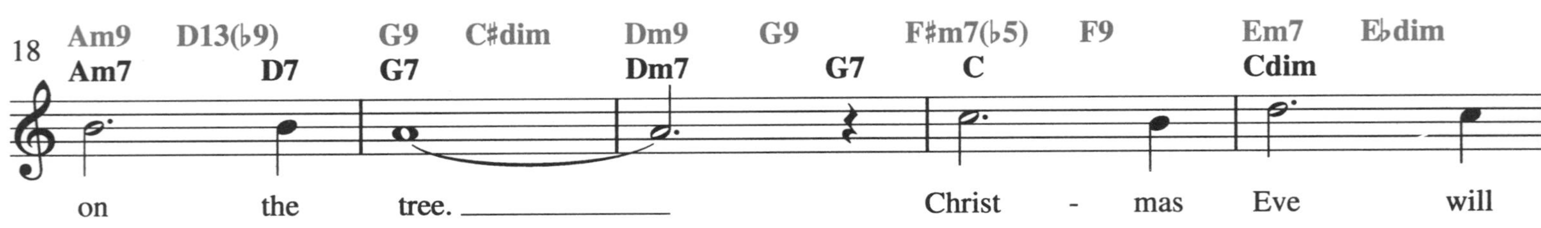

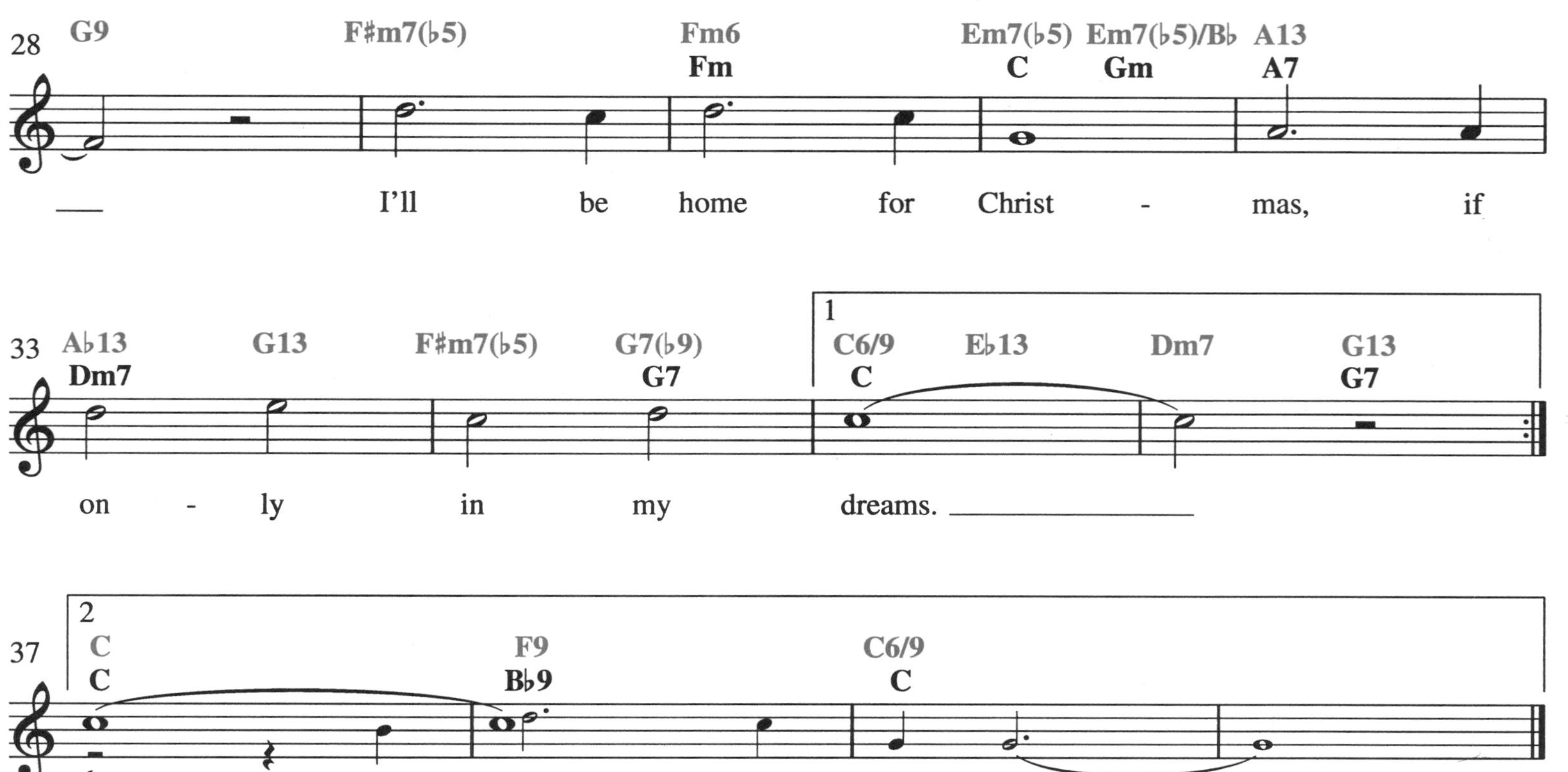

Note that the melody beginning in bar 21 is the same as in bar 5. However, the substitution on the downbeat is different in the two bars. The reason for this is that it is stronger to start the song with a simple tonic chord. Besides, the F♯m7(♭5) comes as a pleasant surprise in bar 21.

IT MUST HAVE BEEN THE MISTLETOE

(Our First Christmas)

By JUSTIN WILDE
and DOUG KONECKY

F(add9)
Dm(add9)
B♭(add9)
Gm(add9)
Em7(♭5) B♭/D C9
loco
Play 8va basso
It

4
F
Gm
F/A
B♭
F(add9)
F(add9)/A
must have been the mis-tle-toe, the la-zy fire, the fall-ing snow, the

6
F/A
Gm
B♭/F
F/A
B♭
C7sus
B♭(add9)
B♭/C
ma-gic in the frost-y air, that feel-ing ev-'ry-where. It

8
F
Dm
Cm7
F9sus
F(add9)
Cm7
E♭/F
must have been the pret-ty lights that glis-tened in the si-lent night, or

10
B♭
Gm
F9
Em7(♭5) A13(♭9)
B♭maj9
E♭9
B♭maj7
Gm7
B♭/C
B♭maj7
may-be just the stars so bright that shined a-bove you. Our first

13
Dm7
Gm7
C9
Fmaj9
F6
Fmaj7
Gm7
C9
Fmaj7
Christ-mas, more than we'd been dream-ing of.

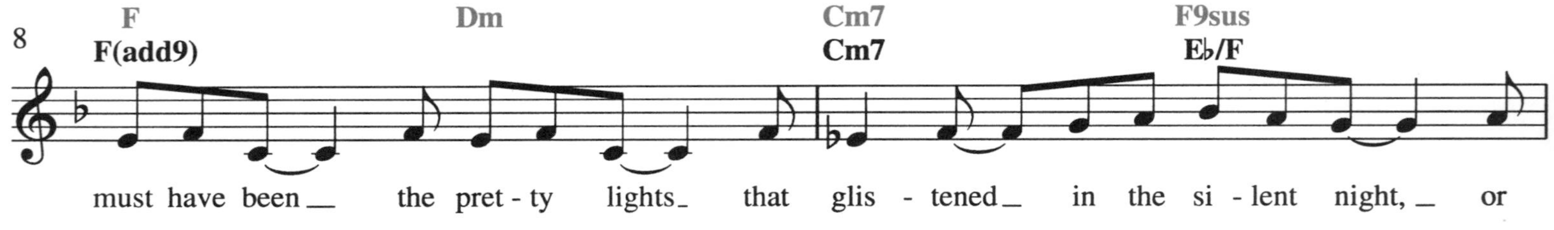

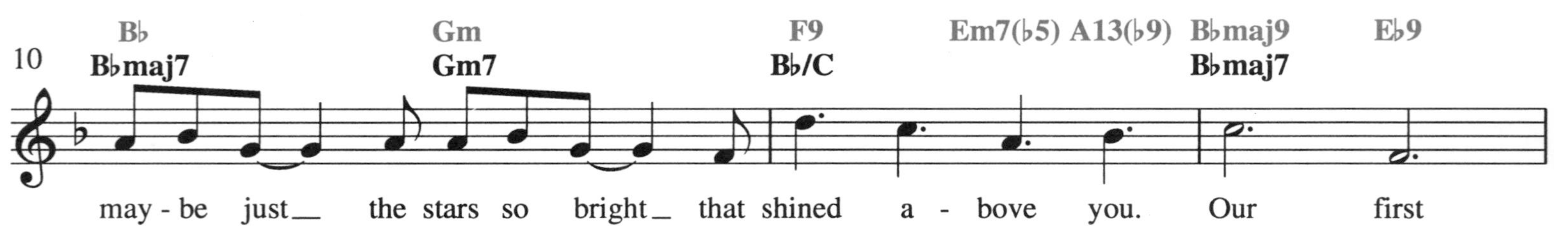

16
B♭m7 E♭9 Cm7 Fm7 B♭7sus B♭7/D
B♭m7 E♭9 Cm7 Fm7 B♭7sus B♭7
Old Saint Nich - 'las had his fin - gers crossed, that

19
B♭maj9/C C13 C7sus F Gm
B♭/C C B♭/C F(add9)
we would fall in love. It could have been the hol - i - day, the

21
F/A B♭ F/A Gm
F(add9)/A B♭(add9)
mid-night ride up - on a sleigh, the coun - try side all dressed in white, that

23
B♭/F F/A B♭ C7sus F Dm
B♭/C F(add9)
cra - zy snow - ball fight. It could have been the stee - ple bell that

25
Cm7 F9sus B♭ Gm F/A B♭maj7 C9
Cm7 E♭/F B♭maj7 Gm7 B♭/C C6
wrapped us up with-in its spell. It on - ly took one kiss to know, it must have been the

28
F(add9) B♭maj9 E♭9 Dm7
F(add9) B♭maj7 Fmaj7
mis - tle - toe. Our first Christ - mas,

31
Gm7 C9 Fmaj9 F6 B♭m7 E♭9
Gm7 C9 Fmaj7 B♭m7 E♭9
more than we'd been dream - ing of. Old Saint

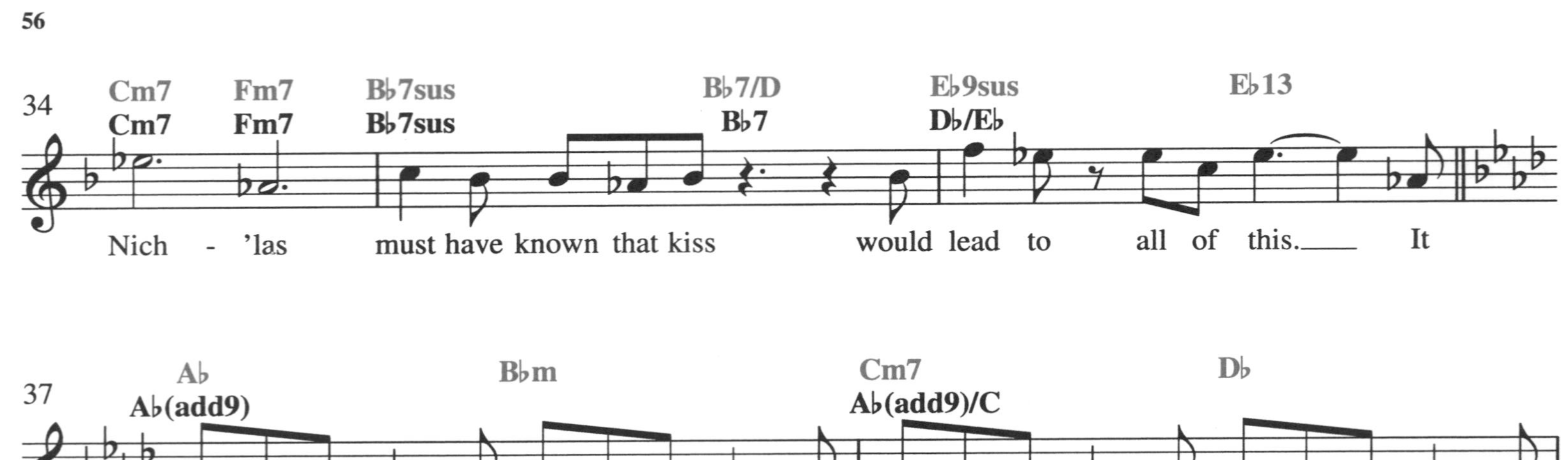
34
Cm7 Fm7 B♭7sus B♭7/D E♭9sus E♭13
Cm7 Fm7 B♭7sus B♭7 D♭/E♭
Nich - 'las must have known that kiss would lead to all of this.___ It

37
A♭ B♭m Cm7 D♭
A♭(add9) A♭(add9)/C
must have been ___ the mis - tle - toe,___ the la - zy fire,___ the fall - ing snow,_ the

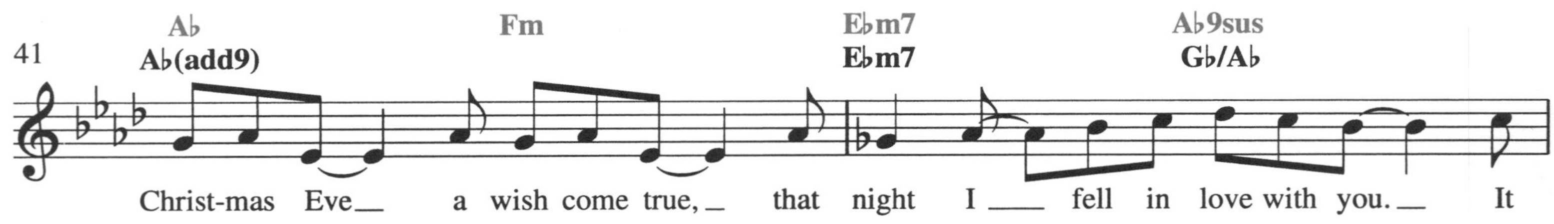
39
Cm7 B♭m D♭/A♭ A♭/C D♭ E♭7sus
D♭(add9) D♭/E♭
mag - ic in ___ the frost - y air,___ that made me love you. On

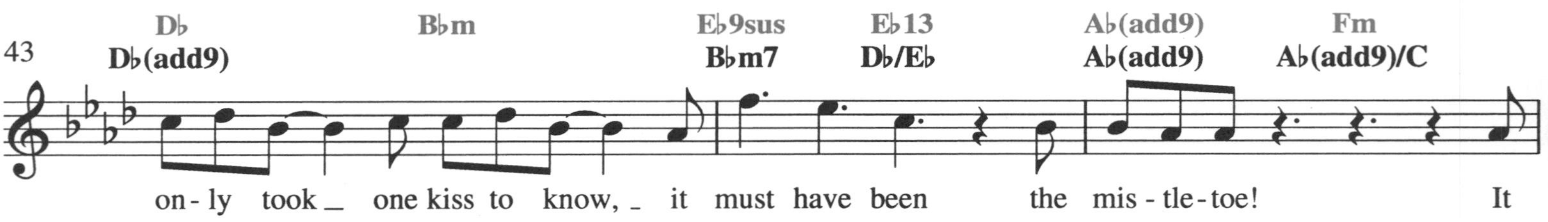
41
A♭ Fm E♭m7 A♭9sus
A♭(add9) E♭m7 G♭/A♭
Christ-mas Eve___ a wish come true,_ that night I ___ fell in love with you.___ It

43
D♭ B♭m E♭9sus E♭13 A♭(add9) Fm
D♭(add9) B♭m7 D♭/E♭ A♭(add9) A♭(add9)/C
on - ly took _ one kiss to know, _ it must have been the mis - tle - toe! It

46
B♭m7 C7 Fm Fm/E Fm/E♭ Fm/D D♭ E♭13
B♭m7 E♭6 Fm Fm(maj7) Fm7 Fm6 B♭m7 D♭/E♭
must have been the mis - tle - toe! It must have been the
49
A♭(add9) Fm(add9) D♭(add9) B♭m C7 F(add9)
A♭(add9)
arp.
mis-tle-toe!
rit.

JINGLE BELLS

IT'S BEGINNING TO LOOK LIKE CHRISTMAS

Words and Music by
MEREDITH WILLSON

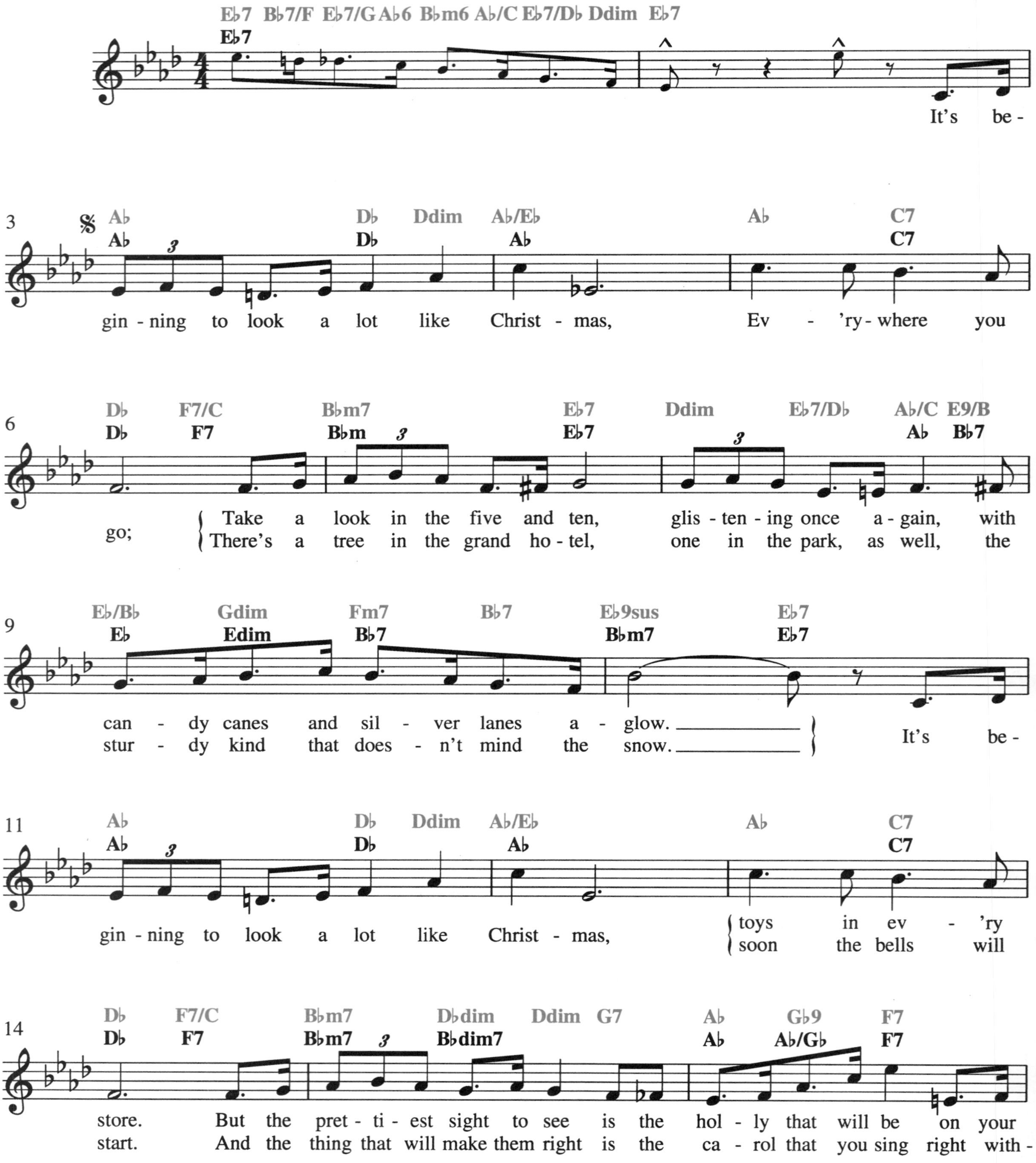

E♭7 B♭7/F E♭7/G A♭6 B♭m6 A♭/C E♭7/D♭ Ddim E♭7
E♭7
It's be -

3 A♭ D♭ Ddim A♭/E♭ A♭ C7
A♭ D♭ A♭ C7
gin - ning to look a lot like Christ - mas, Ev - 'ry - where you

6 D♭ F7/C B♭m7 E♭7 Ddim E♭7/D♭ A♭/C E9/B
D♭ F7 B♭m E♭7 A♭ B♭7
go; { Take a look in the five and ten, glis - ten - ing once a - gain, with
There's a tree in the grand ho - tel, one in the park, as well, the

9 E♭/B♭ Gdim Fm7 B♭7 E♭9sus E♭7
E♭ Edim B♭7 B♭m7 E♭7
can - dy canes and sil - ver lanes a - glow. ______ } It's be -
stur - dy kind that does - n't mind the snow. ______

11 A♭ D♭ Ddim A♭/E♭ A♭ C7
A♭ D♭ A♭ C7
gin - ning to look a lot like Christ - mas, { toys in ev - 'ry
soon the bells will

14
D♭ F7/C B♭m7 D♭dim Ddim G7 A♭ G♭9 F7
D♭ F7 B♭m7 B♭dim7 A♭ A♭/G♭ F7
store. But the pret - ti - est sight to see is the hol - ly that will be on your
start. And the thing that will make them right is the ca - rol that you sing right with -

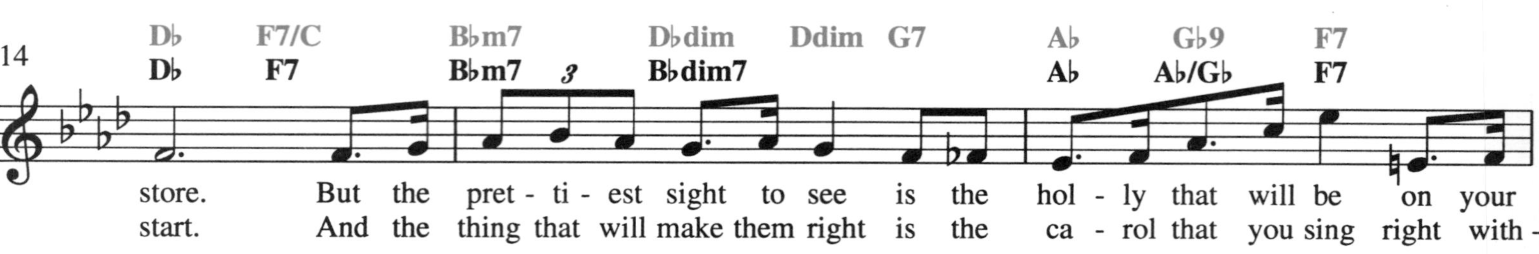

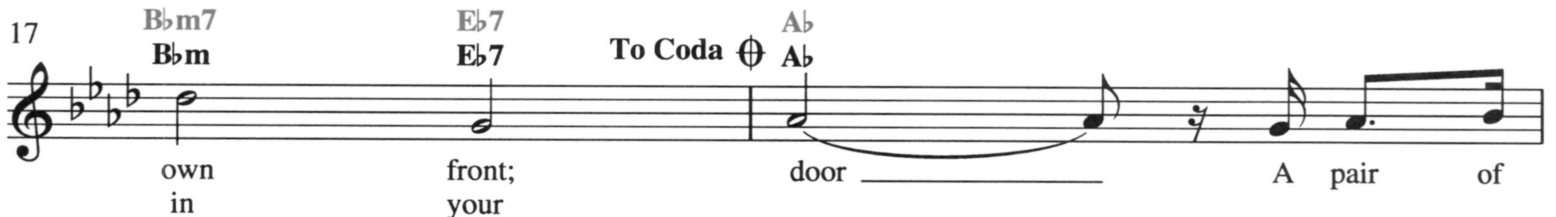

The introduction can be played with the melody and bass line only:

JINGLE-BELL ROCK

Words and Music by JOE BEAL
and JIM BOOTHE

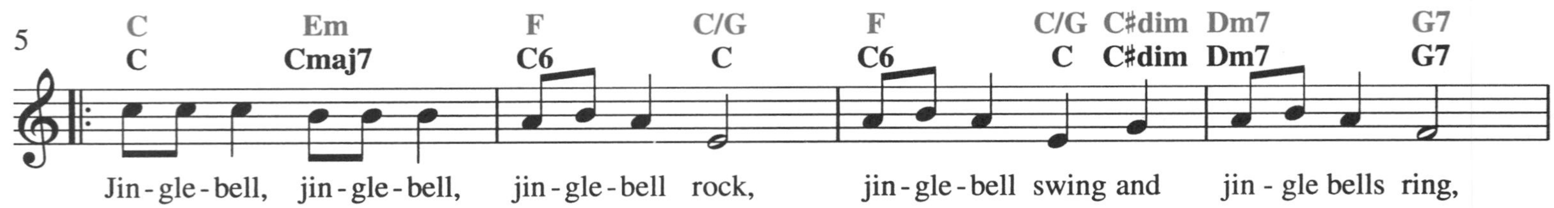

24
C C7(♯5) F Am7 D7 G7 D9
C7(♯5) F D7 G7 G9
way, jin - gle - bell __ time __ is a swell time __ to go glid - in' in a
28
G7 D7/A G7/B G7 C Em F C/G F C/G B♭13
G7 C Cmaj7 C6 C C6 C B♭7
one - horse sleigh. Gid - dy - up, jin - gle-horse pick up your feet jin - gle a - round the
32
A7 G/B Cm6 A7/C♯ Dm7 B♭9 Am7 D13 G7
A7 F Fm D7 G7
clock; Mix and min - gle in a jin - gl - in' beat that's the jin - gle - bell
36
1
C
C
rock.
2
F♯m7(♭5) B7 Em E♭9 D7 G7 C
D7 G7 D7 G7 C
that's the jin - gle - bell, that's the jin - gle - bell rock.

LET IT SNOW! LET IT SNOW! LET IT SNOW!

Words by SAMMY CAHN
Music by JULE STYNE

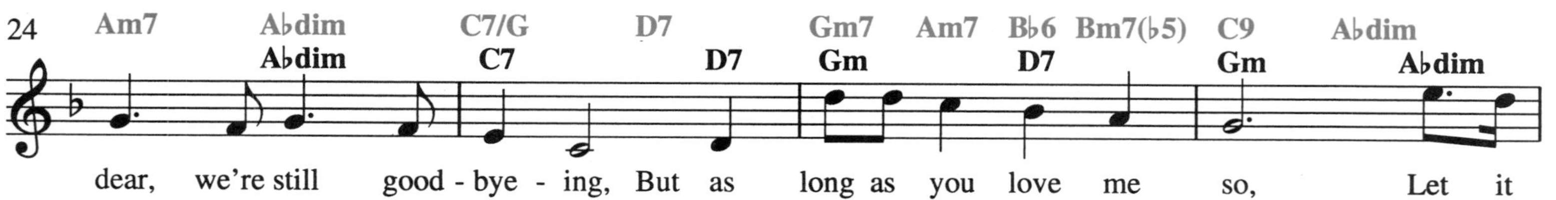
24
Am7 A♭dim C7/G D7 Gm7 Am7 B♭6 Bm7(♭5) C9 A♭dim
A♭dim C7 D7 Gm D7 Gm A♭dim
dear, we're still good - bye - ing, But as long as you love me so, Let it

28
Am7 D7 G9 C13 F [D7] C7
C7 F D.S. al Coda
snow! Let it snow! Let it snow! Oh the
CODA
Am7 D7 G9 F♯dim
C7
snow! Let it snow! Let it

31
G9 B♭m6 Am6 A♭dim Am7 D7 G9 C13 F
F
snow! Let it snow! Let it snow! Let it snow! Let it snow!

LET'S HAVE AN OLD FASHIONED CHRISTMAS

Lyric by LARRY CONLEY
Music by JOE SOLOMON

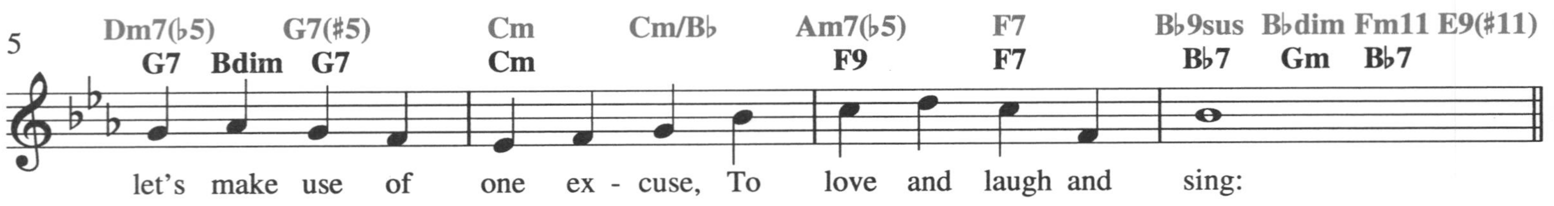

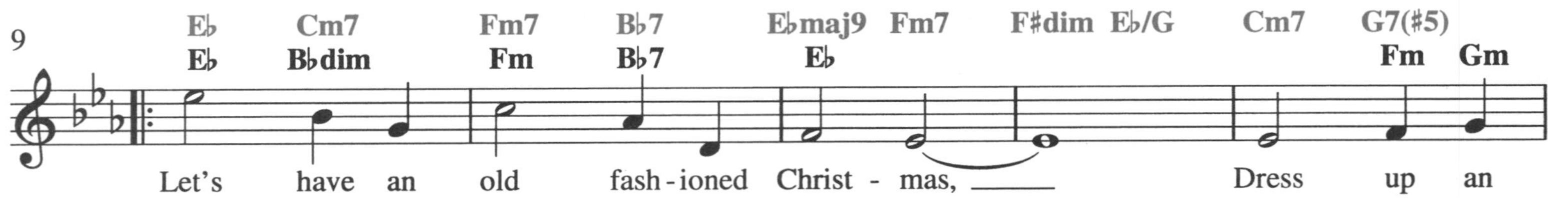

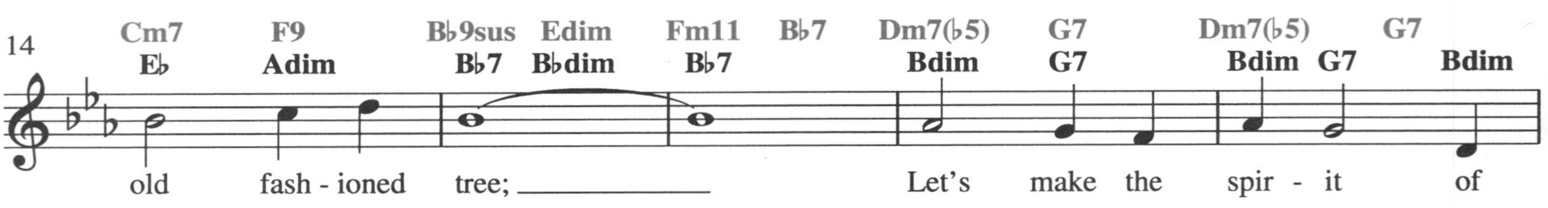

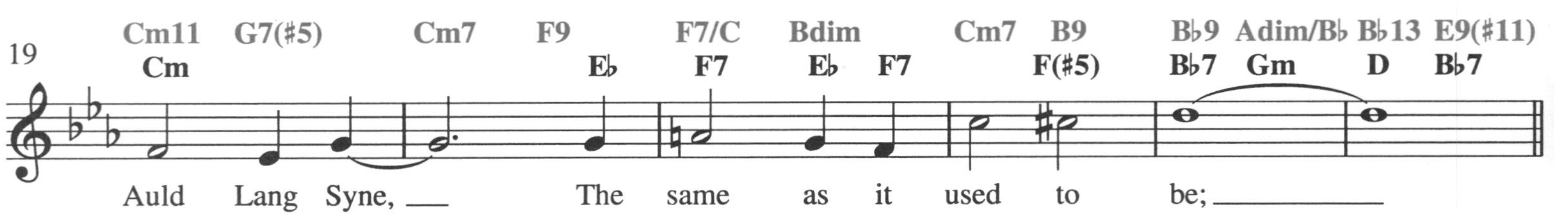

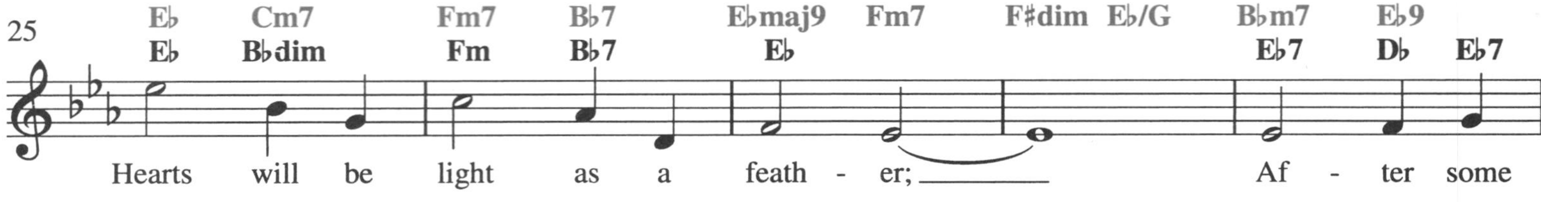

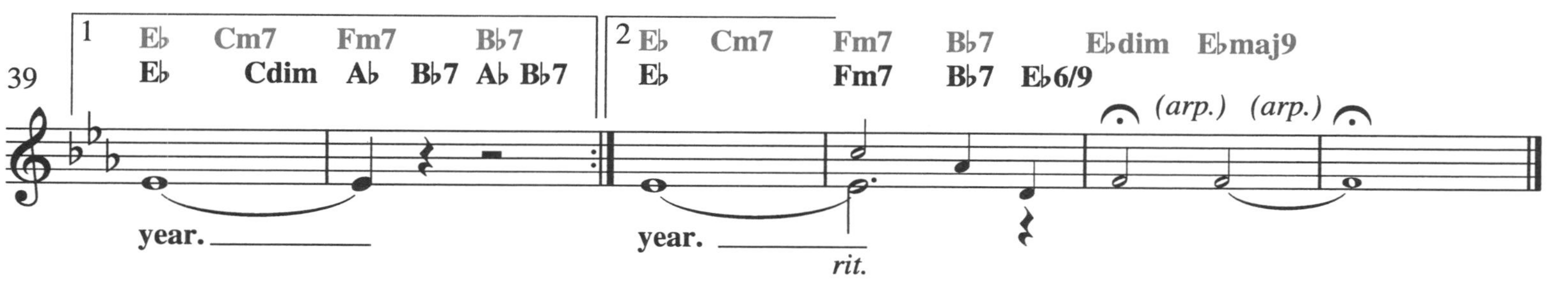

The substitutions of the last two bars of the song (43-44) allow for some effective voice leading of the inner voices. The outer voices remain the same (F's on top; E♭'s on bottom) while the inner voices resolve nicely (C to D; A to B♭; F# to G).

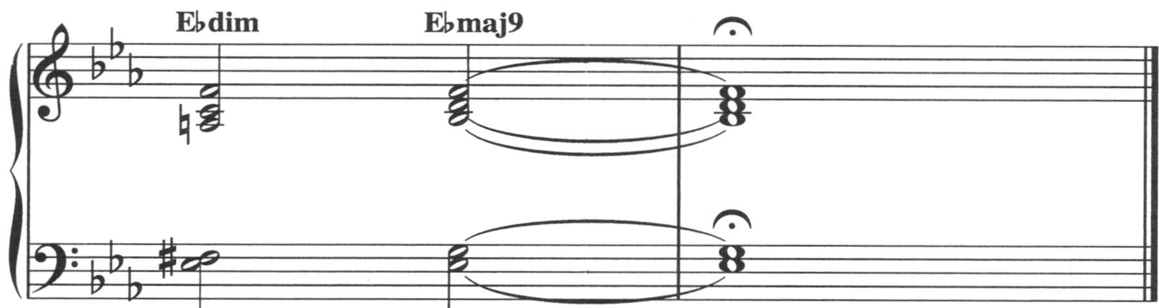

A MARSHMALLOW WORLD

Words by CARL SIGMAN
Music by PETER DE ROSE

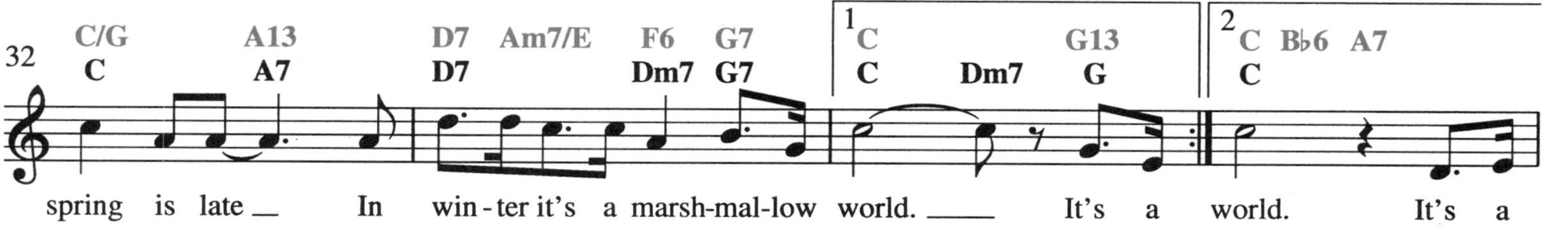

1. Try playing the first 8 bars of the tune (bars 3-10) only with melody and bass (no chords). The bass line is very important. Then begin playing the chords at bar 11.
2. The ending tag (bars 36-40) may be played rubato.

MISTER SANTA

Additional Lyrics

2. Mister Santa, dear old Saint Nick
Be awful careful and please don't get sick
Put on your coat when breezes are blowin'
And when you cross the street look where you're goin'.
Santa, we (I) love you so,
We (I) hope you never get lost in the snow.
Take your time when you unpack,
Mister Santa don't hurry back.

3. Mister Santa, we've been so good
We've washed the dishes and done what we should.
Made up the beds and scrubbed up our toesies,
We've used a kleenex when we've blown our nosesies.
Santa look at our ears, they're clean as whistles,
We're sharper the shears
Now we've put you on the spot,
Mister Santa brings us a lot.

1. In both the Intro and Ending, play the notes (cue size) staccato and let them ring. This figure is commonly used when this song is played.
2. The last chord (substitute) is a bit of a surprise, yet doesn't sound completely out of context. Here is a suggested voicing for the final two chords:

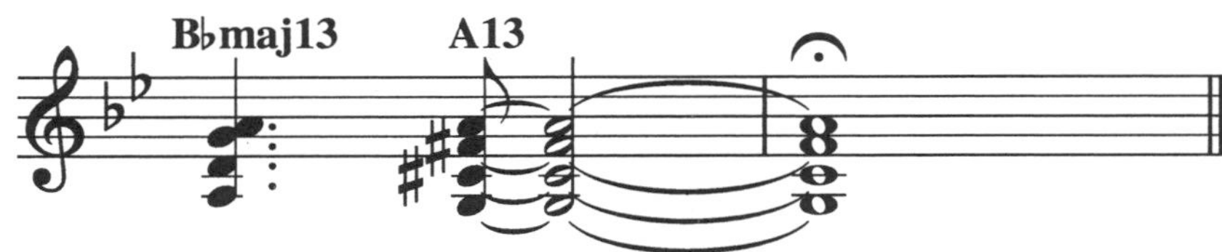

MY FAVORITE THINGS

Lyrics by OSCAR HAMMERSTEIN II
Music by RICHARD RODGERS

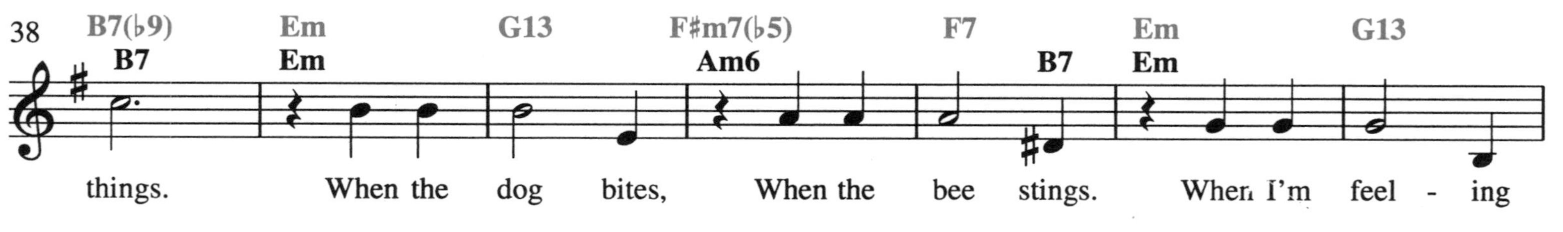
38
B7(♭9)
B7
Em
Em
G13
F♯m7(♭5)
Am6
F7
B7
Em
Em
G13
things. When the dog bites, When the bee stings. When I'm feel - ing

45
Cmaj9
C
C6
Cmaj7
C♯m7(♭5)
G/D
A7
A7/C♯
Cm6
Bm7
G C G
sad. I sim - ply re - mem - ber my fa - vor - ite things and then I don't

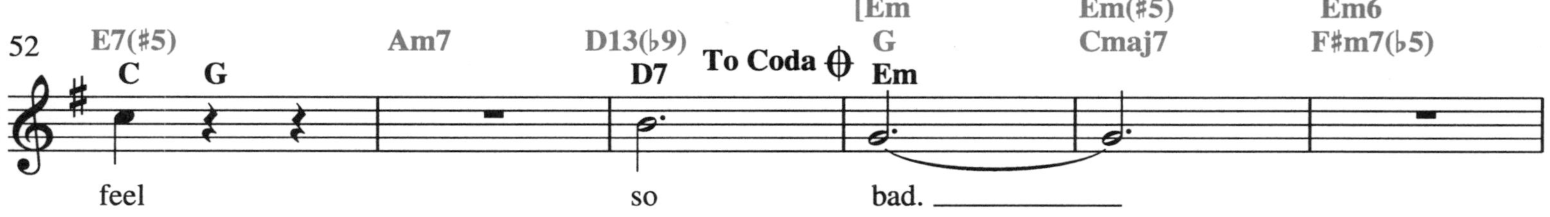
52
E7(♯5)
C G
Am7
D13(♭9)
D7
To Coda
[Em
G
Em
Em(♯5)
Cmaj7
Em6
F♯m7(♭5)
feel so bad.

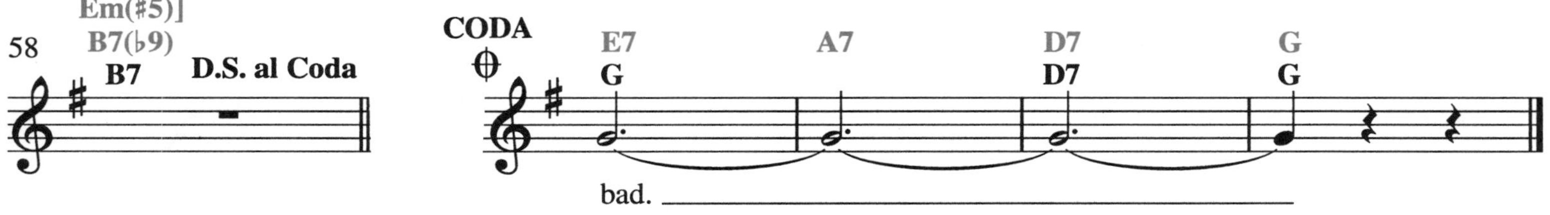
58
Em(♯5)]
B7(♭9)
B7
D.S. al Coda
CODA
E7
G
A7
D7
D7
G
G
bad.

THE NIGHT BEFORE CHRISTMAS SONG

Music by JOHNNY MARKS
Lyrics adapted by JOHNNY MARKS
from CLEMENT MOORE'S Poem

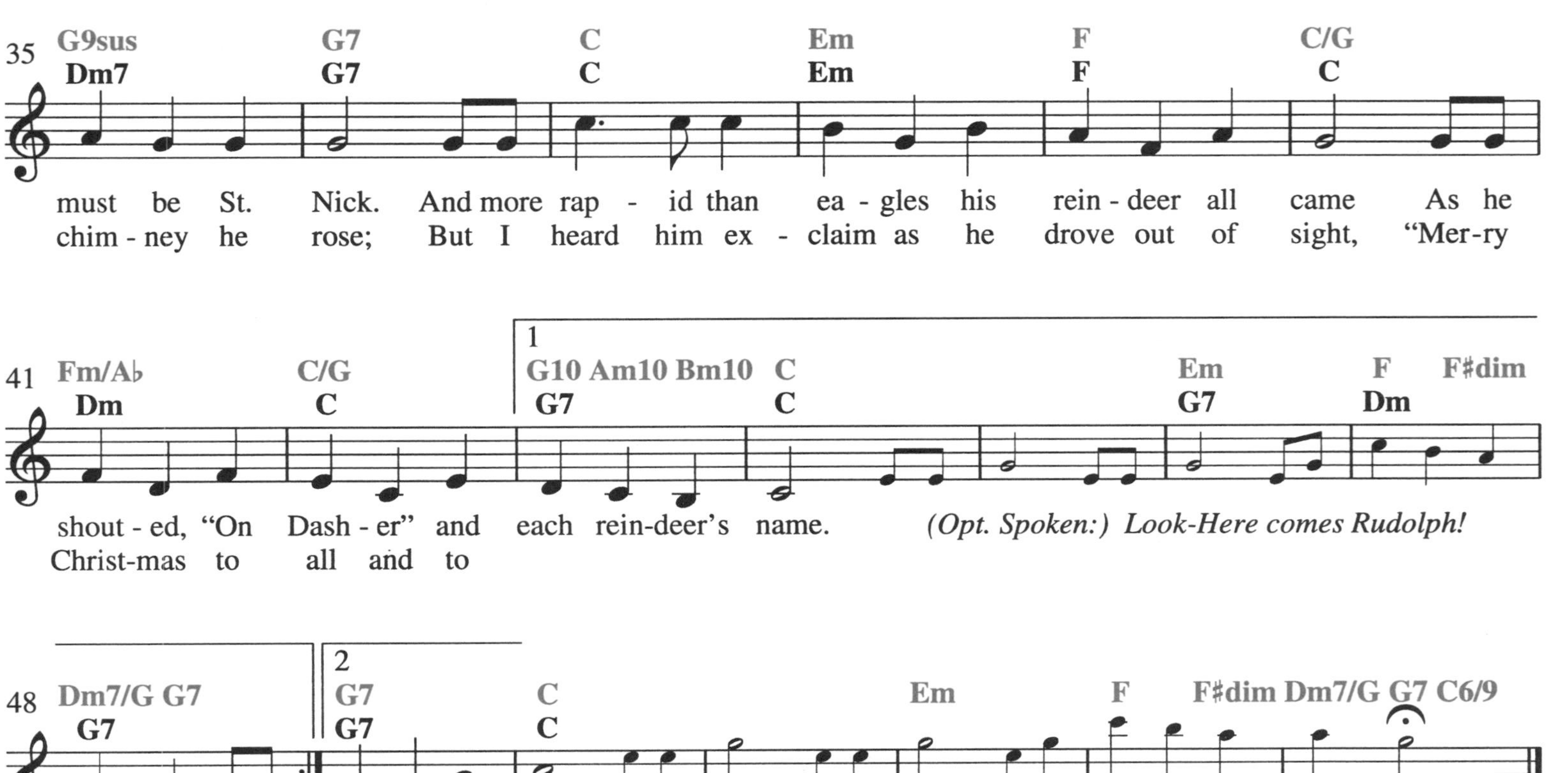
35
G9sus G7 C Em F C/G
Dm7 G7 C Em F C
must be St. Nick. And more rap - id than ea - gles his rein - deer all came As he
chim - ney he rose; But I heard him ex - claim as he drove out of sight, "Mer-ry
41
Fm/A♭ C/G G10 Am10 Bm10 C Em F F♯dim
Dm C G7 C G7 Dm
1
shout - ed, "On Dash - er" and each rein-deer's name.
Christ-mas to all and to
(Opt. Spoken:) Look-Here comes Rudolph!
48
Dm7/G G7 G7 C Em F F♯dim Dm7/G G7 C6/9
G7 G7 C
2
And so all a Good Night!"
rit.

NUTTIN' FOR CHRISTMAS

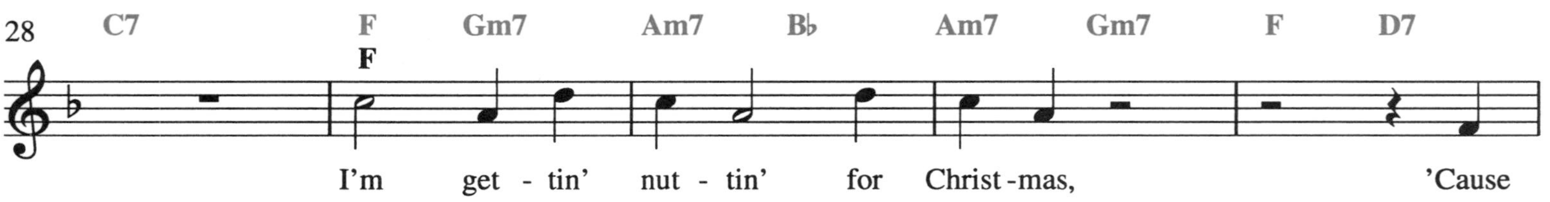

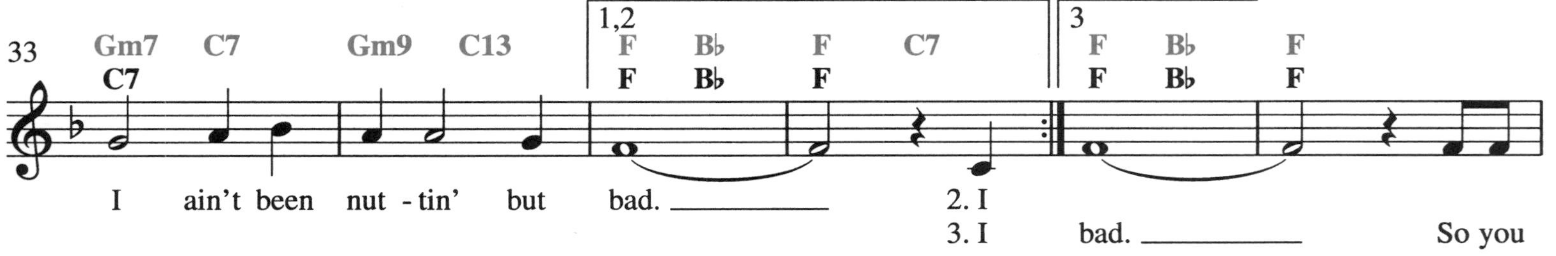

At bar 45, try playing this bassline (contrary motion).

O CHRISTMAS TREE

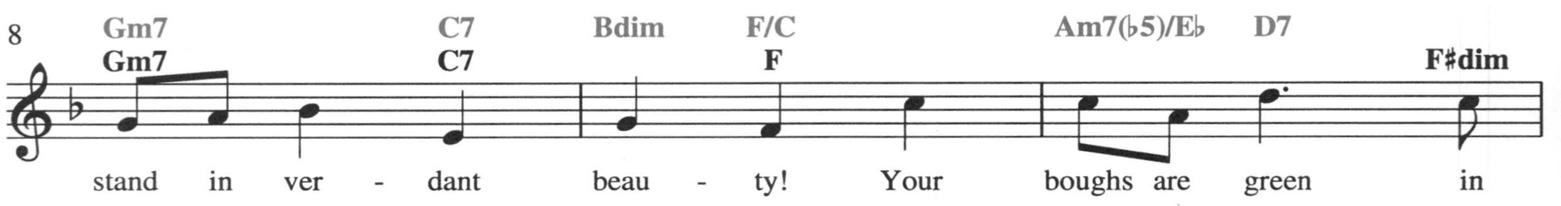

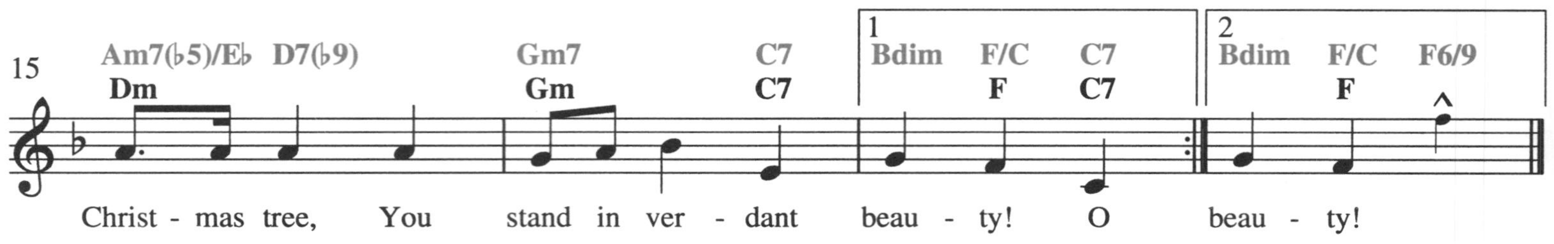

O COME, ALL YE FAITHFUL

O HOLY NIGHT

C
C
Em
F
F
O Ho - ly night ___ the stars are bright - ly
Tru - ly He taught us to love one an -
6
C/E F C/G Fm/A♭ Am Fm/A♭ C/G G7 C
C G C
shin - ing, it is the night of the dear Sav - ior's birth; ___
oth - er, His law is love, and His gos - pel is peace; ___
11
Em F C/E F
F C
___ Long lay the world ___ in sin and er - ror pin -
___ Chains shall He break for the slave is our broth -
16
C7/G B♭dim Em/B F♯m7(♭5) B7 Em
C7 Em/B B7 Em
ing, till He ap - peared and the soul felt its worth. ___ A
er, and in His name all op - pres - sion shall cease. ___ Sweet
21
Dm7 G7 C Am C/G C/E Dm7
G7 C G7
thrill of hope the wea - ry soul re - joic - es, for yon - der
hymns of joy in grate - ful cho - rus raise we, let all with -
26
G7 C Am Em Am Am/G F♯m7(♭5) B7
C Am
breaks a new and glo - rious morn; Fall ___ on your
in us praise His ho - ly name; Christ ___ is the

31 Em Dm/F Am Am/G F♯m7(♭5)
Em Dm Am
knees, ___ oh, hear ___ the an - gel voic - es! O
Lord, ___ oh, praise ___ His name for - ev - er! His

37 C/G G7/F C/E F C/G G7
C G7 C/E F C G7
night ___ di - vine ___ o night ___ when Christ was
pow'r ___ and glo - ry ev - er - more pro -

43 C 1 G G/F E Fmaj7 F6
C G G7 C F
born! ___ O night ___ O ho - ly
claim! ___ His

49 C/G G7 C 2 G G/F
C G7 C G G7
night O night di - vine! ___ pow'r ___ and

55 C/E Fmaj9 Fm(maj7) C/G G7 C
C/E F C G7 C
glo - ry ___ ev - er - more pro - claim! ___

For an introduction, try arpeggiating the C chord. For example:

This pattern can be continued throughout as an accompaniment.

OLD TOY TRAINS

Words and Music by
ROGER MILLER

21
F D7 G7 C7 F9 B♭6 Bdim C7 Gm7/D C7/E
F C B♭ C
— lit-tle toy — tracks, — lit-tle toy — drums — com-in' from a sack, car-ried by a

25
F F7/E♭ B♭/D B♭m6/D♭ F/C C9
F F7 B♭ F C7
man dressed in white and red. Lit-tle boy — don't — you think it's time you were in

28
1
F B♭6 F/A Gm7 F B♭6 F/A F♯dim
F B♭6 F B♭6 F B♭6 F
bed? So close your
2
Freely
F N.C.
F
bed? Lit-tle boy — don't —

33
a tempo
F C7 F B♭6 F/A Gm7 F
C7 F B♭6 F B♭6 F
— you think it's time you were in bed?

PRETTY PAPER

Words and Music by
WILLIE NELSON

32
Cm/E♭
G/D
G
D7
D7
G Am10 B♭m10 Bm10 D7
G
and in the midst of the laugh - ter he cries.
Pret - ty

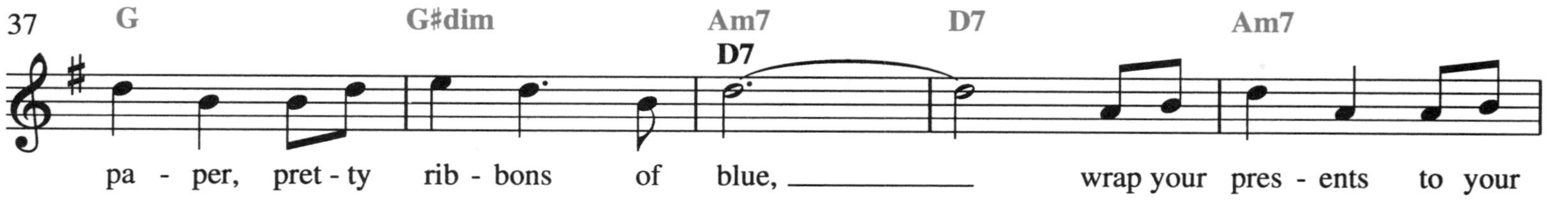
37
G
G♯dim
Am7
D7
D7
Am7
pa - per, pret - ty rib - bons of blue,
wrap your pres - ents to your

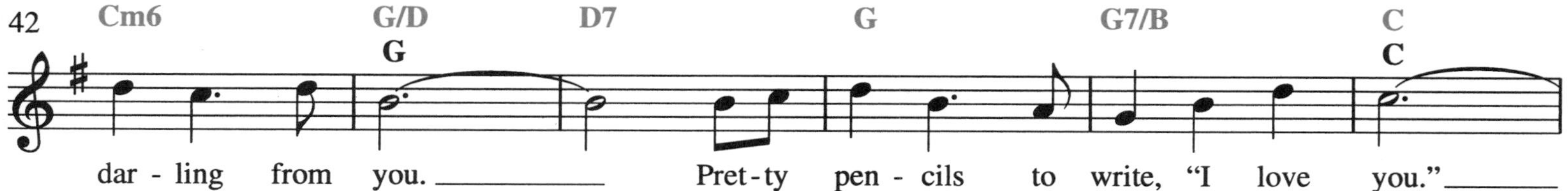
42
Cm6
G/D
G
D7
G
G7/B
C
C
dar - ling from you.
Pret - ty pen - cils to write, "I love you."

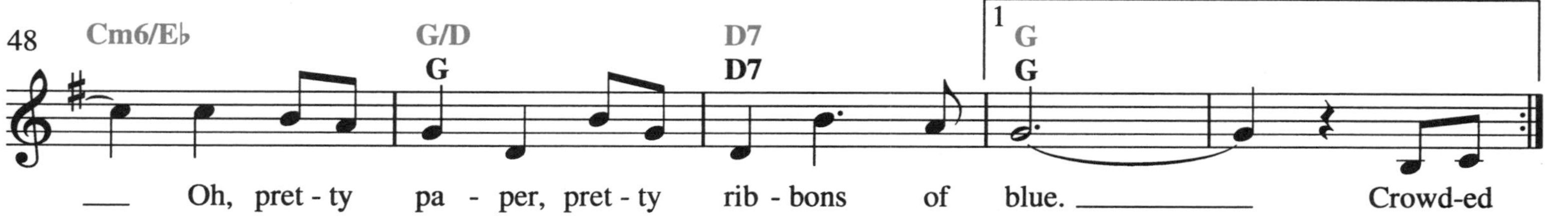
48
Cm6/E♭
G/D
G
D7
D7
1
G
G
Oh, pret - ty pa - per, pret - ty rib - bons of blue.
Crowd - ed

53
2
G10 Am10 Bm10
G
Cm6
C
G/D
G
D7
D7
G
G
Oh, pret - ty pa - per, pret - ty rib - bons of blue.

ROCKIN' AROUND THE CHRISTMAS TREE

Music and Lyrics by
JOHNNY MARKS

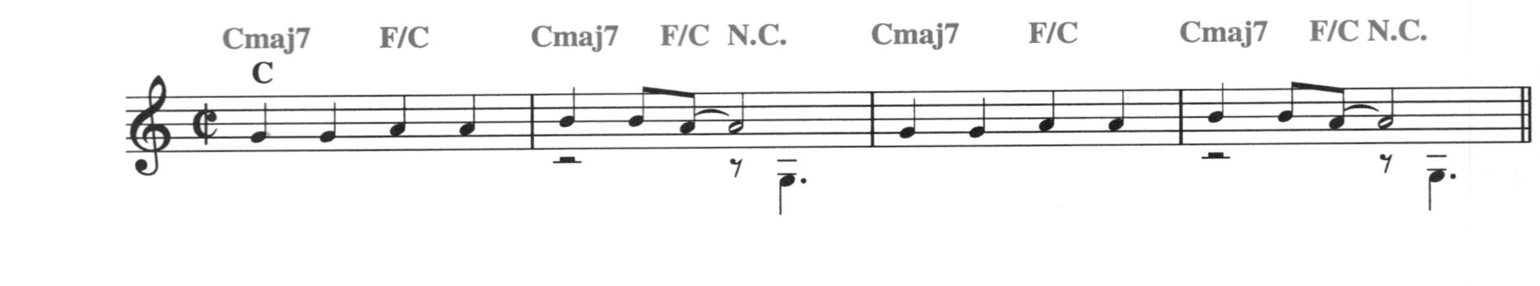

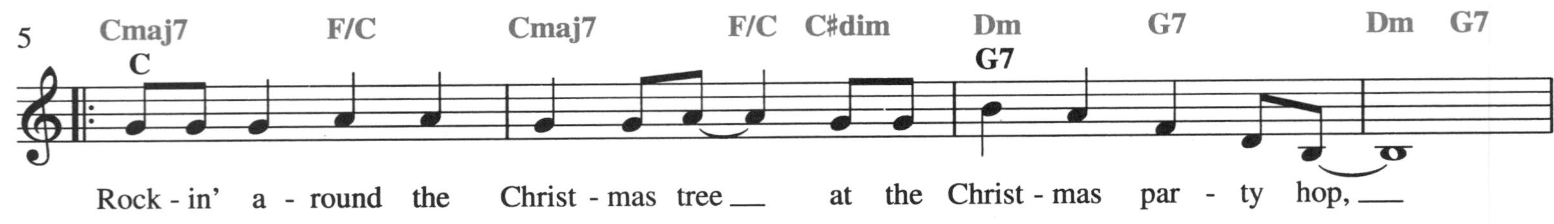

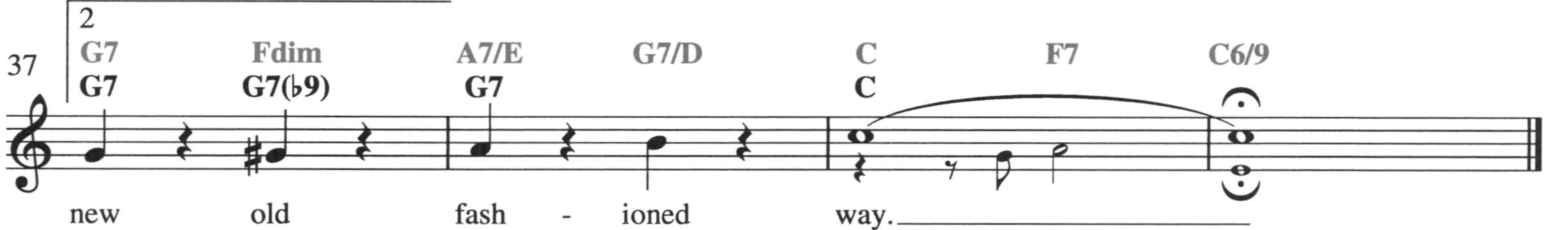

In bars 5-20, you might try anticipating the chord on beat 3 of every other measure. For example:

This rhythm figure will work in bars 29-36 as well.

RUDOLPH, THE RED-NOSED REINDEER

Music and Lyrics by
JOHNNY MARKS

24
G/D
E7
Am7(♭5)
D7
G7
A♭13
G9
C
Fmaj7
Gmaj7
G♯dim
Am
Am7
D7
G7
C
nose so bright, won't you guide my sleigh to - night?"
Then how the rein - deer

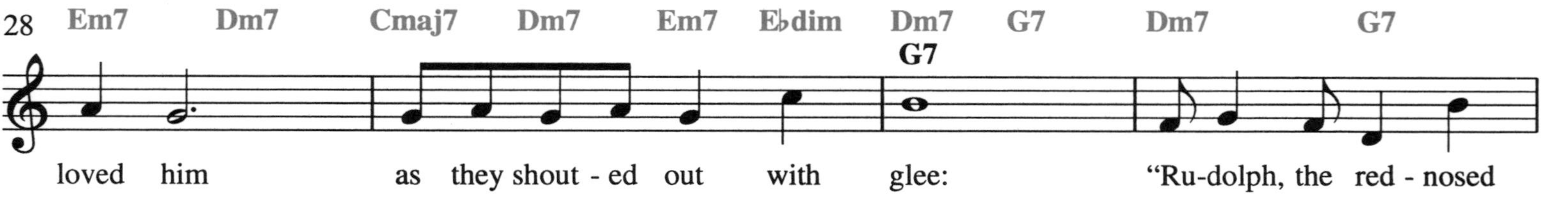
28
Em7
Dm7
Cmaj7
Dm7
Em7
E♭dim
Dm7
G7
Dm7
G7
G7
loved him as they shout - ed out with glee:
"Ru-dolph, the red - nosed

32
Dm7
C♯dim
Dm7
E♭dim
Edim
F♯dim
G7
F13(♯11)
C
F9
C
F
C6/9
C♯dim
G7
C
rein - deer, you'll go down in his - to - ry!"

SANTA BABY

By JOAN JAVITS, PHIL SPRINGER
and TONY SPRINGER

The vamp in bars 39 and 40 is optional and can be used for vocal or instrumental ad libs. This arrangement would also work if these two bars are skipped completely.

SILENT NIGHT

1. Depending on the context, it might be best to stick with the original chords when this is sung, especially if it is intended to be hymn-like.
2. Bars 14 and 15 should be played rather dramatically, taking time to pause on the last quarter note of the melody in bar 15.

TOYLAND

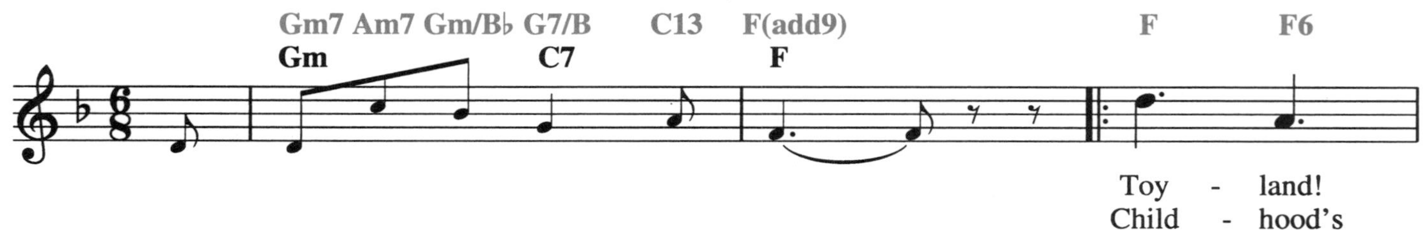

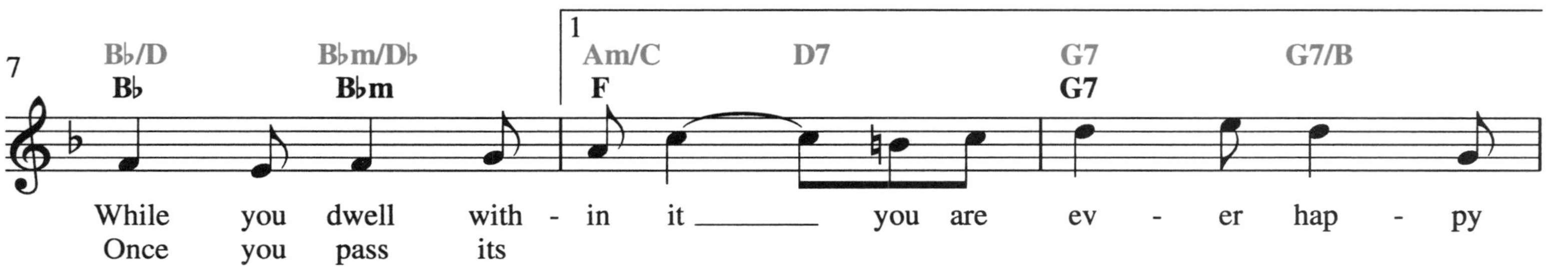

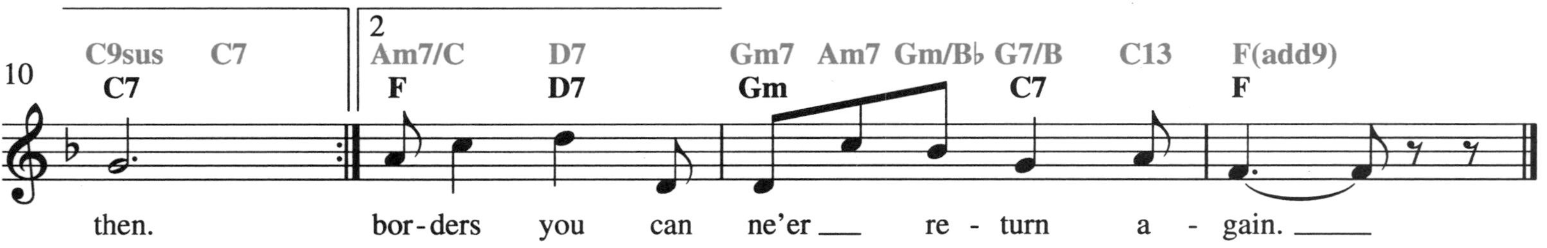

When playing the substitute chords, notice the voice leading of the chords in bar 6:

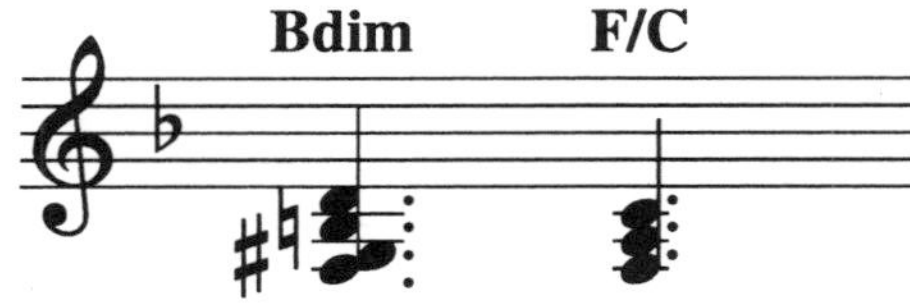

The two inner voices of the Bdim chord move chromatically in contrary motion to the melody (while the F stays constant).

SILVER AND GOLD

Music and Lyrics by
JOHNNY MARKS

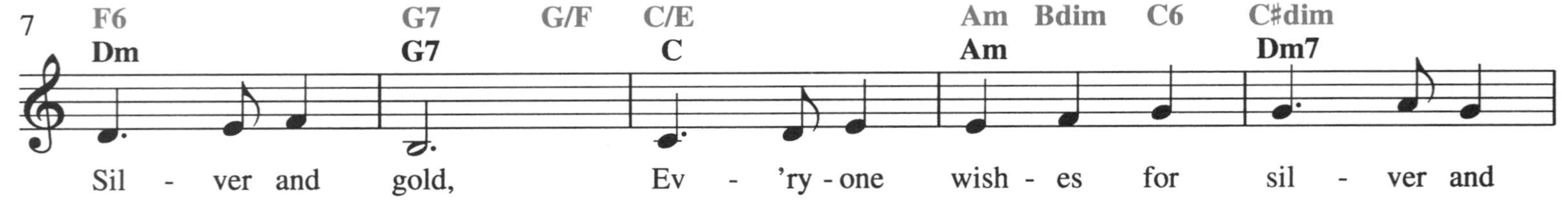

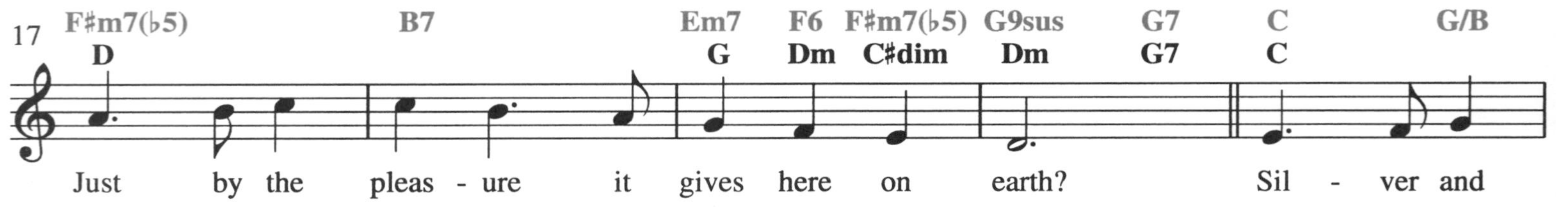

Note that both the intro and ending are based on the rhythm of the melody.

THAT CHRISTMAS FEELING

Words and Music by BENNIE BENJAMIN
and GEORGE WEISS

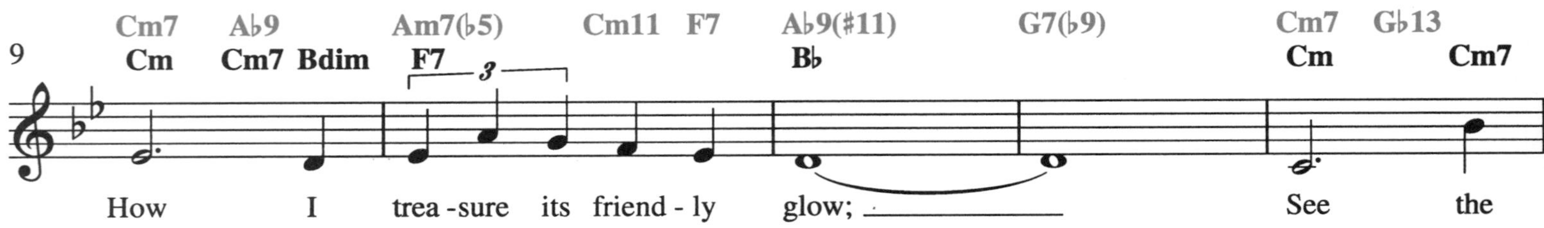

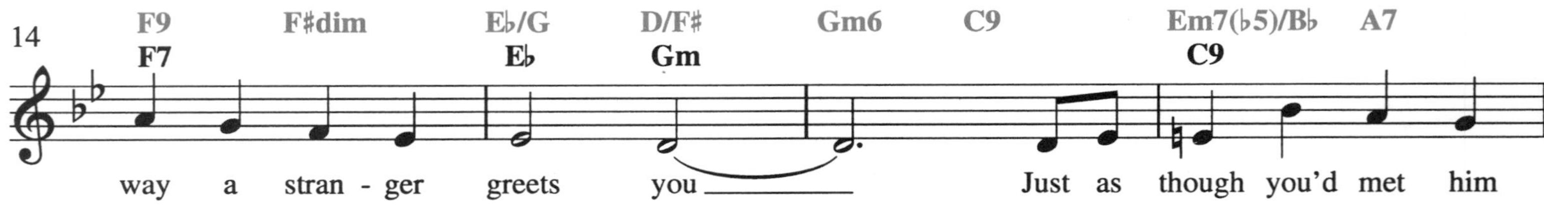

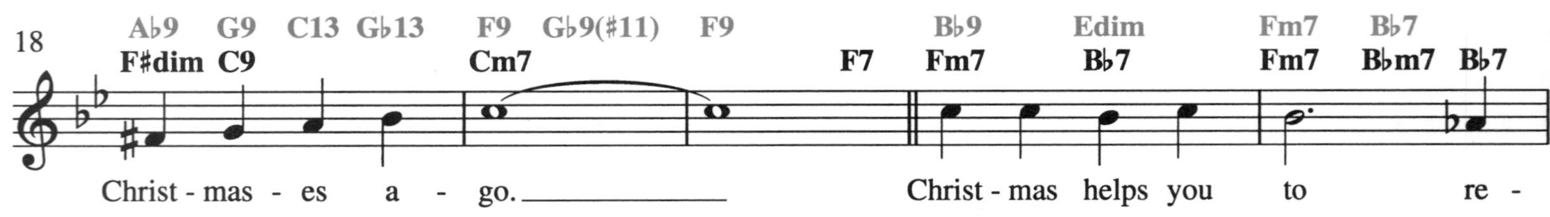

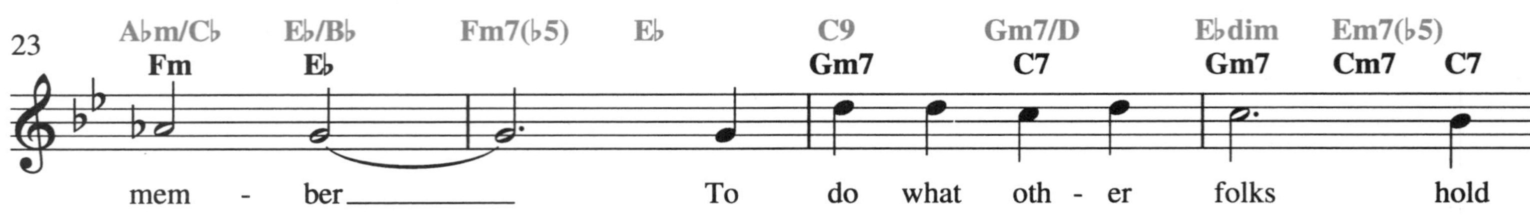

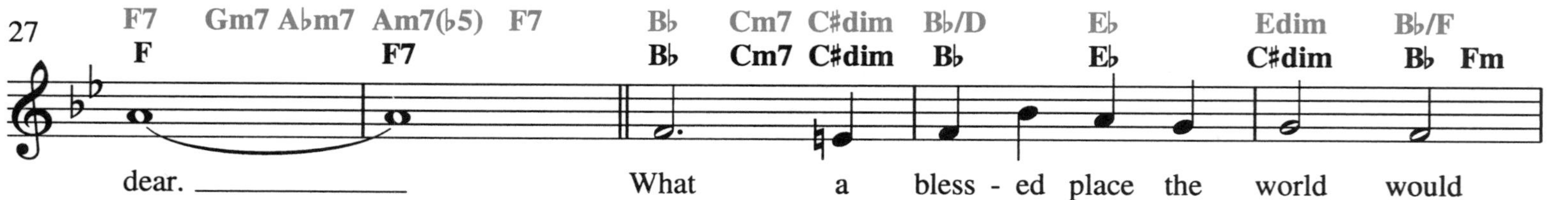
27
F7 Gm7 A♭m7 Am7(♭5) F7
F F7
B♭ Cm7 C♯dim B♭/D E♭ Edim B♭/F
B♭ Cm7 C♯dim B♭ E♭ C♯dim B♭ Fm
dear.
What a bless - ed place the world would

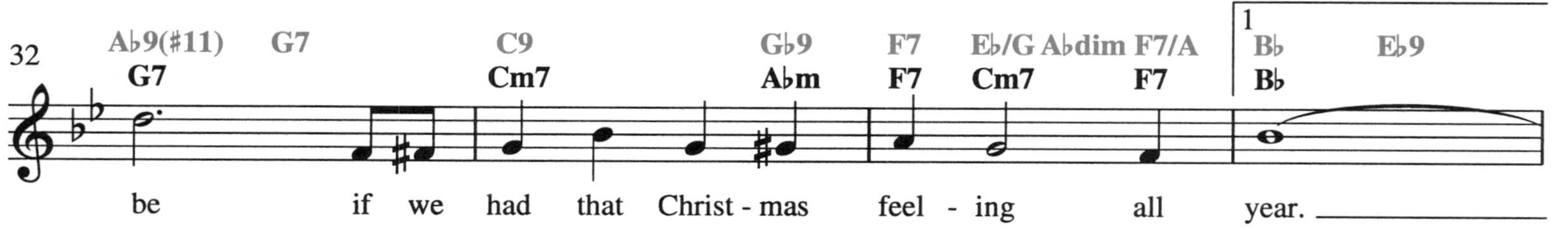
32
A♭9(♯11) G7 C9 G♭9 F7 E♭/G A♭dim F7/A
G7 Cm7 A♭m F7 Cm7 F7
1
B♭ E♭9
B♭
be if we had that Christ - mas feel - ing all year.

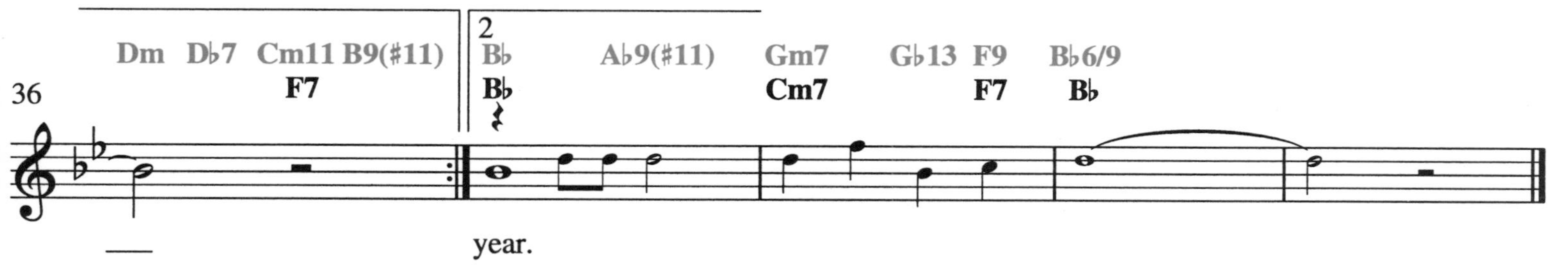
36
Dm D♭7 Cm11 B9(♯11)
F7
2
B♭ A♭9(♯11) Gm7 G♭13 F9 B♭6/9
B♭ Cm7 F7 B♭
year.

THERE IS NO CHRISTMAS LIKE A HOME CHRISTMAS

Words by CARL SIGMAN
Music by MICKEY J. ADDY

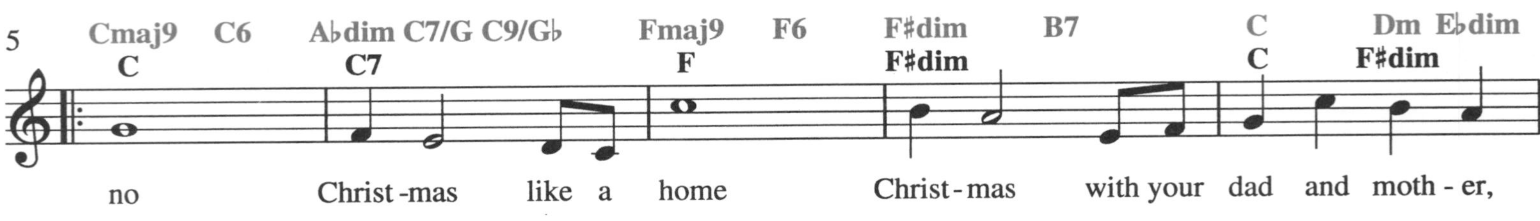

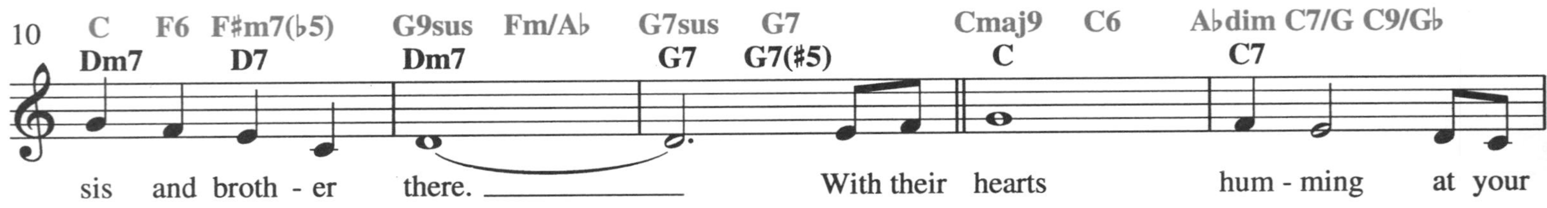

29
Cmaj9 C6
C
Ab dim C7/G C9/Gb
C7
Fmaj9 F6
F
F#dim B7
F#dim
C Dm Ebdim
Em7 Fmaj7 Ebdim
no Christ-mas like a home Christ-mas for that's the time of

34
C F6 F#m7(b5) G7
Dm7 G7
1
C F#dim G9sus G7
C6 Fmaj7 Em7 Dm7 Em7 Dm7 G7
2
C Dm Ebdim
C6 Fmaj7 Em7 Dm7
year all roads lead home. There is home.

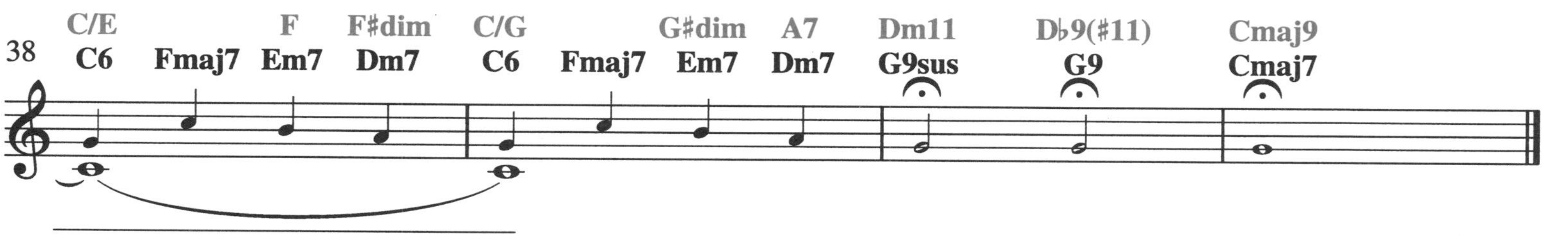
38
C/E F F#dim C/G G#dim A7 Dm11 Db9(#11) Cmaj9
C6 Fmaj7 Em7 Dm7 C6 Fmaj7 Em7 Dm7 G9sus G9 Cmaj7

UP ON THE HOUSETOP

The last time through the song, play bar 18 with deliberation and with a tenuto on beat 3. Then, play the last two bars quickly.

WONDERFUL CHRISTMASTIME

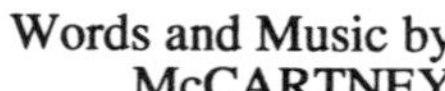
Words and Music by
McCARTNEY

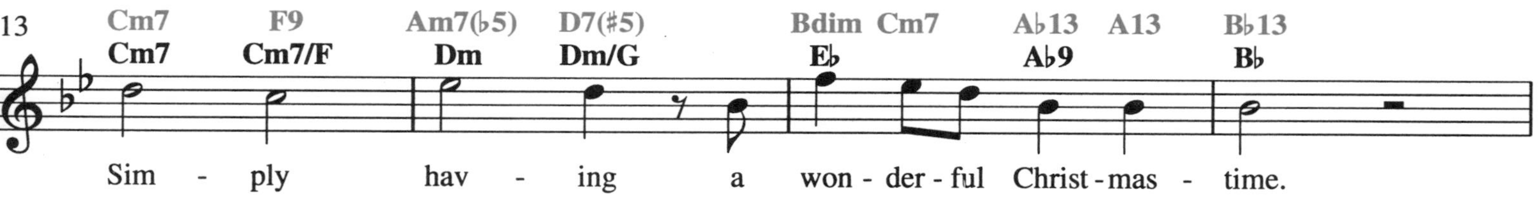

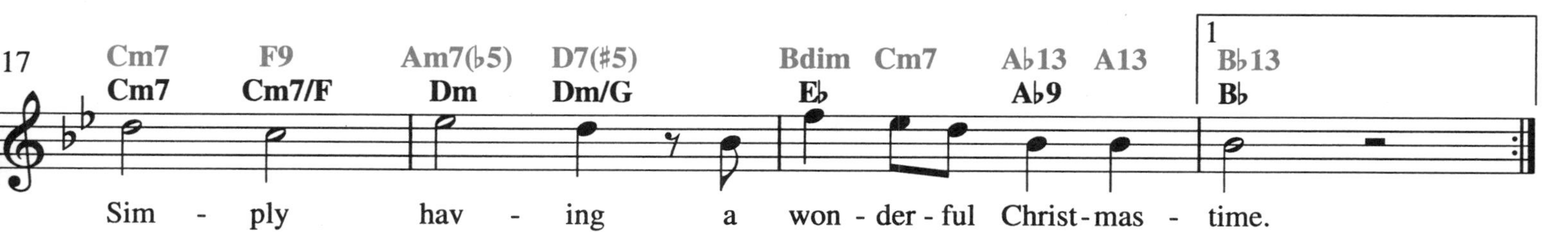

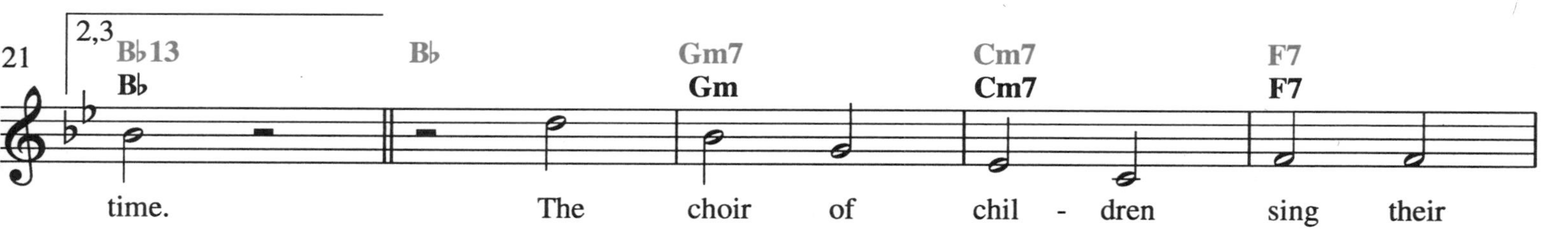

To Coda
26
B♭ Gm7 Cm7 F7 B♭6/9
B♭ Gm Cm7 F7 B♭
song. (They prac - tised all year long.) Ding
31
E♭
E♭
dong, ding dong. Ding dong, ding. Ooh
36
Cm7 F9sus B♭
Cm7 E♭/B♭ E♭ B♭/D
Ooh
Do do do
41
B♭(♯5) B♭6 B♭7 Cm9 F9 Am7(♭5) D7(♯5)
B♭ Cm7 Cm7/F Dm Dm/G
do do do do
We're sim - ply hav - ing a
46
Bdim Cm7 A♭13 A13 B♭13 Cm9 F9 Am7(♭5) D7(♯5)
E♭ A♭9 B♭ Cm7 Cm7/F Dm Dm/G
won - der - ful Christ - mas - time.
Sim - ply hav - ing a
50
Bdim Cm7 A♭13 A13 B♭13
E♭ A♭9 B♭
D.S. al Coda
won - der - ful Christ - mas - time.
CODA
B♭ D/B♭ E♭6/9/B♭ D/B♭
B♭ E♭/B♭ B♭
Ding dong, ding
54
E♭6/9/B♭ D/B♭ E♭6/9/B♭ D/B♭ E♭6/9/B♭ D/B♭ E♭6/9/B♭ D/B♭ F9sus
E♭/B♭ B♭ E♭/B♭ B♭ E♭/B♭ B♭ E♭/B♭ B♭ F7
dong, ding dong, ding dong, ding dong, ding dong, dong,

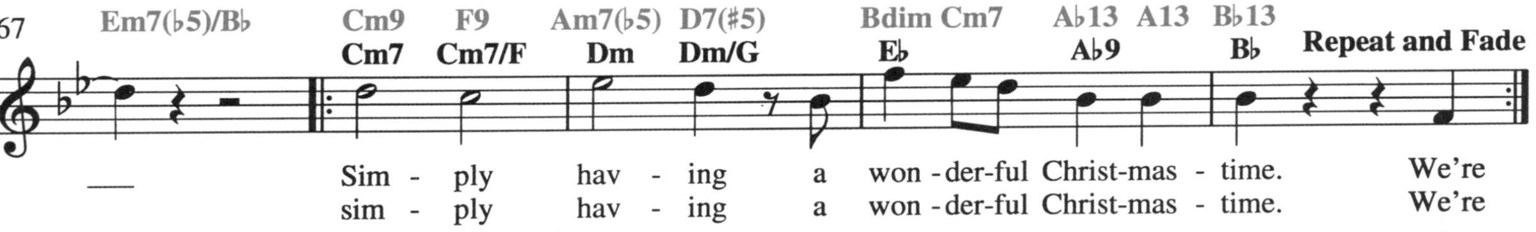

1. The substitute chords in bars 5-13 suggest a chromatic counter-melody: F - F# - G - A♭ - G - F# - F - E
2. In bars 13-16, try beginning the phrase softly and crescendo to bar 16. Do this each time this phrase is repeated, as in bars 17-20 and elsewhere in the song.

WE NEED A LITTLE CHRISTMAS

Music and Lyric by
JERRY HERMAN

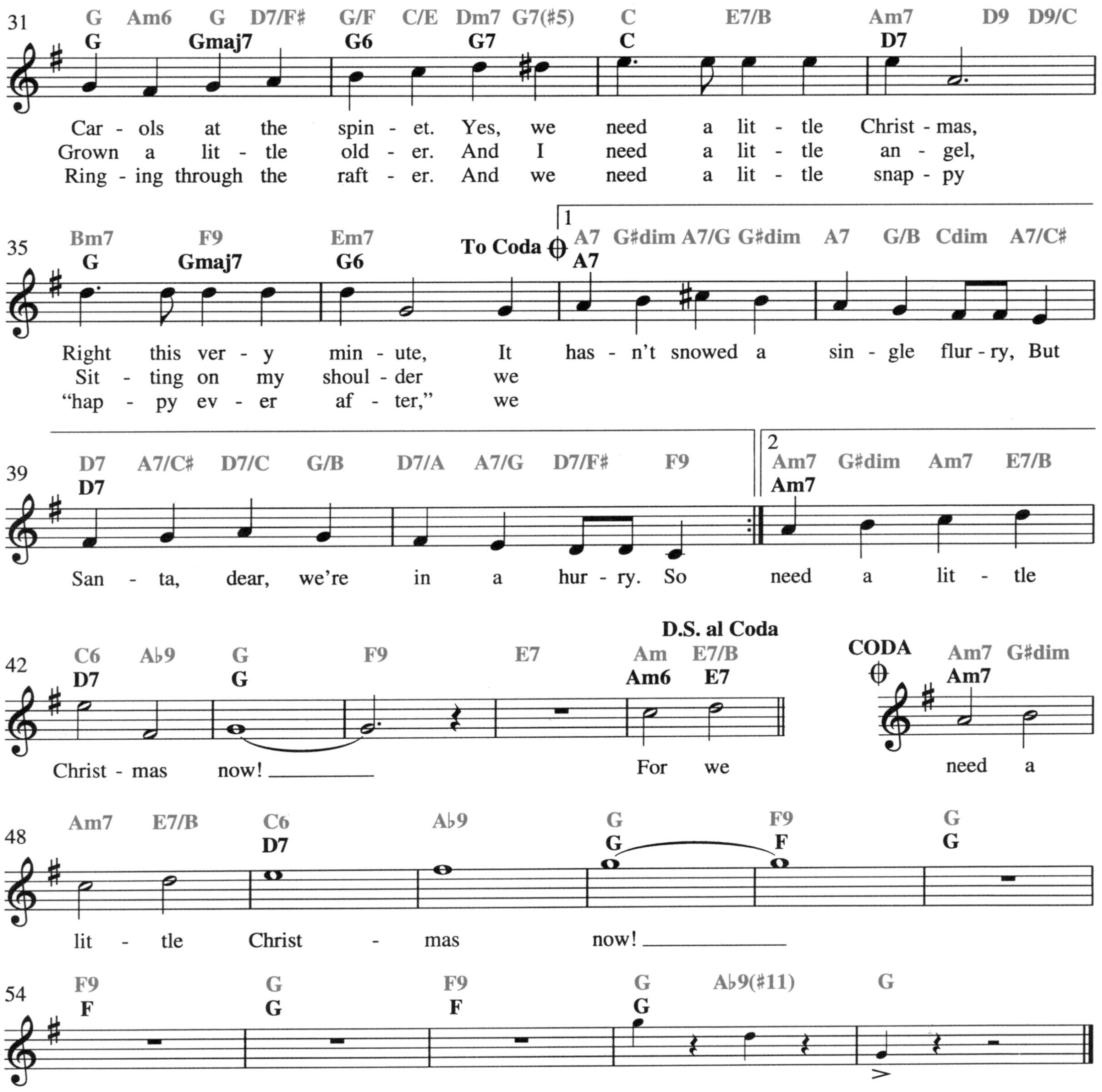
31
G Am6 G D7/F# G/F C/E Dm7 G7(#5) C E7/B Am7 D9 D9/C
G Gmaj7 G6 G7 C D7
Car - ols at the spin - et. Yes, we need a lit - tle Christ - mas,
Grown a lit - tle old - er. And I need a lit - tle an - gel,
Ring - ing through the raft - er. And we need a lit - tle snap - py
35
Bm7 F9 Em7 A7 G#dim A7/G G#dim A7 G/B Cdim A7/C#
G Gmaj7 G6 To Coda A7
1
Right this ver - y min - ute, It has - n't snowed a sin - gle flur - ry, But
Sit - ting on my shoul - der we
"hap - py ev - er af - ter," we
39
D7 A7/C# D7/C G/B D7/A A7/G D7/F# F9 Am7 G#dim Am7 E7/B
D7 Am7
2
San - ta, dear, we're in a hur - ry. So need a lit - tle
42
D.S. al Coda
C6 Ab9 G F9 E7 Am E7/B
D7 G Am6 E7
Christ - mas now! For we
CODA
Am7 G#dim
Am7
need a
48
Am7 E7/B C6 Ab9 G F9 G
D7 G F G
lit - tle Christ - mas now!
54
F9 G F9 G Ab9(#11) G
F G F G

1. The introduction is the same as the 1st ending. At a very bright tempo, it might be best to play only the melody note with the bass note for these 4 bars. Another option would be to play the melody along with a note a sixth below (as well as the bass note):

A7 G#dim A7/G G#dim A7 G/B Cdim A7/C# D7 A7/C# D7/C G/B D7/A A7/G D7/F# F9
A7 D7
etc.

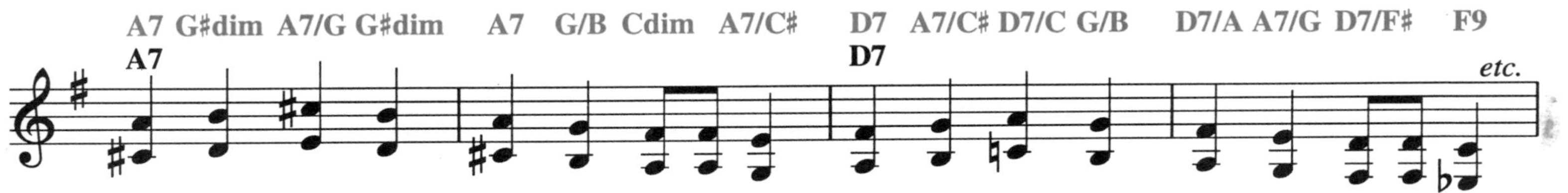

2. The substitutions in bars 5-10 are based on a whole step parallel chord concept. This concept is used again in the ending.

WHAT ARE YOU DOING NEW YEAR'S EVE?

Words and Music by
FRANK LOESSER

22
F Bm7(♭5) E7 | Am | F#m7(♭5) | Bm7 | E7(♭9) | Am | F#m7(♭5)
F | E7(♭9) | Am | D7 | Fm | B♭9 | Am
Eve. May-be I'm cra - zy to sup - pose I'd ev - er be the

26
Bm7 | E7(♭9) | Am | Am(#5) | Am6 | Am7
Bm7(♭5) | B♭9 | Am | D9
one you chose Out of the thou - sand in - vi - ta - tions

29
B♭6 | G7/B | C7 Gm7/D E♭dim C7/E | F | F7/A | B♭m6 | E♭9
G7 | G9 | C7 | F#dim C7 | F | E♭7
you'll re - ceive. Ah, but in case I stand one lit - tle chance,

33
F | F7/E♭ | B♭/D | B♭m6/D♭ | F/C | D9
F | B♭ | B♭m | F | Dm7
Here comes the jack - pot ques - tion in ad - vance, What are you do - ing

To Coda ⊕ **D.S. al Coda**

36
G7 | G7/B | C7 | C9sus C13 | F | C7
G7 | C9 | Gm9 C7(♭9) | F Bdim B♭m C7
New Year's, New Year's Eve?

CODA ⊕
C7 | A7/C#
C7 | A7/C#
New Year's

40
Dm Dm/C | Bm7(♭5) | E7 | Am7 | D7 | G7 | C7(♭9) | F(add9)
Dm Dm/C | Bm7(♭5) | E7 | Am7 | D7 | G7 | C7(♭9) | F
Eve? New Year's Eve?

Here is a counter-melody figure to play in bars 7 and 8 (when playing the substitutions):

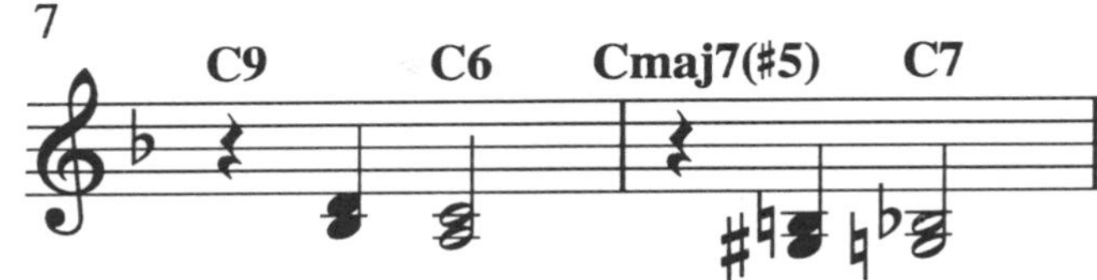

WHAT CHILD IS THIS?

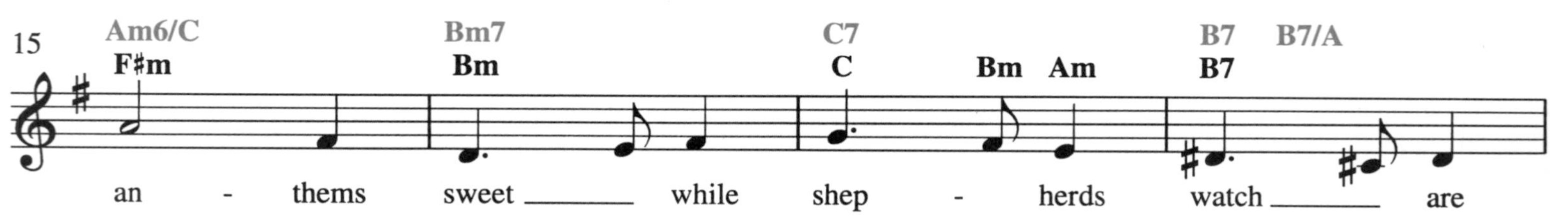

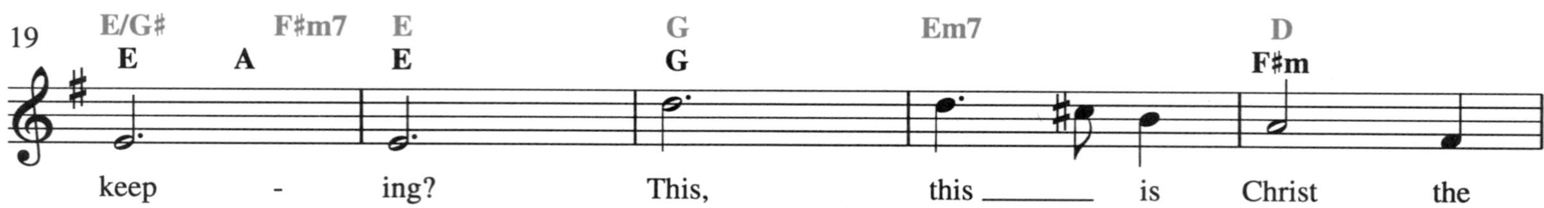

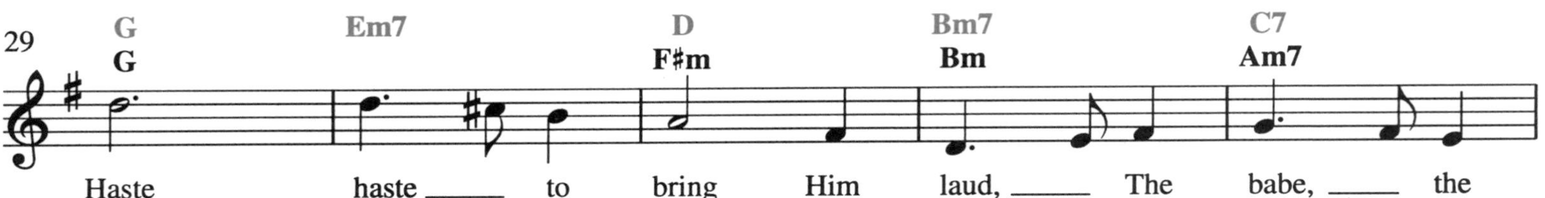

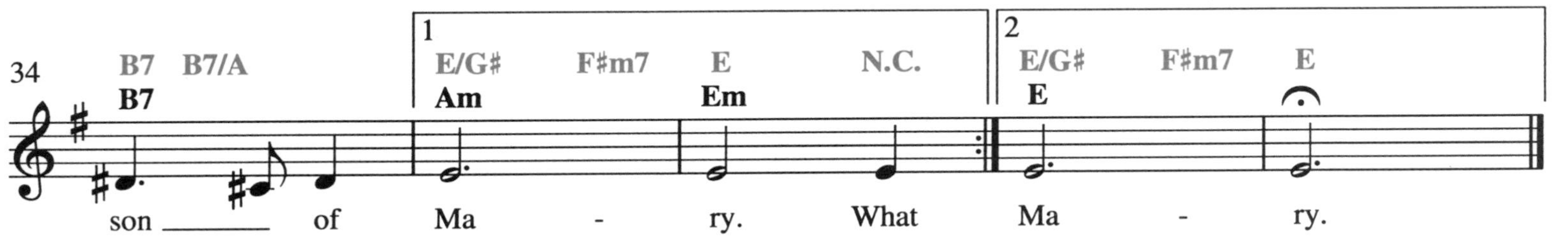

The substitutions in this song work particularly well if it is played in a Jazz Waltz style. If not, the original chords might be preferred if this is played in the traditional Carol style.

YOU'RE ALL I WANT FOR CHRISTMAS

Words and Music by GLENN MOORE
and SEGER ELLIS

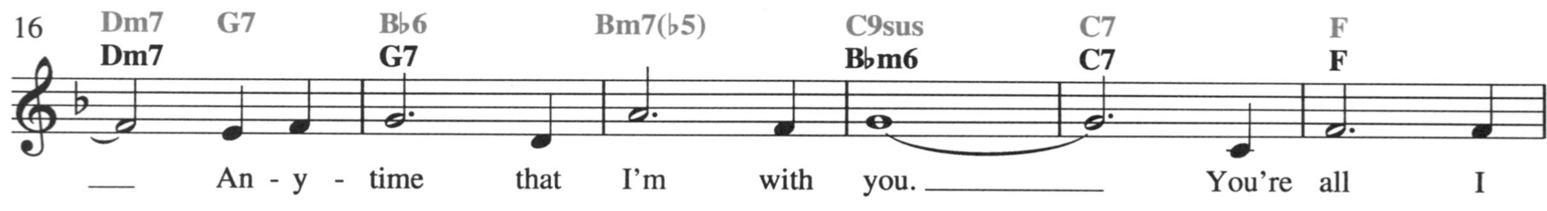

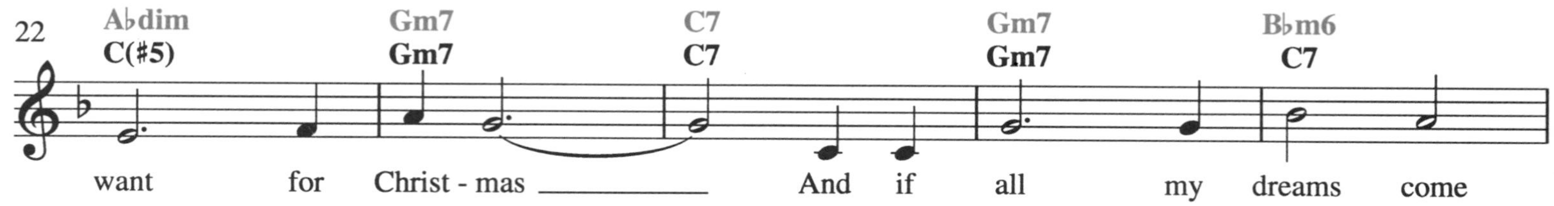

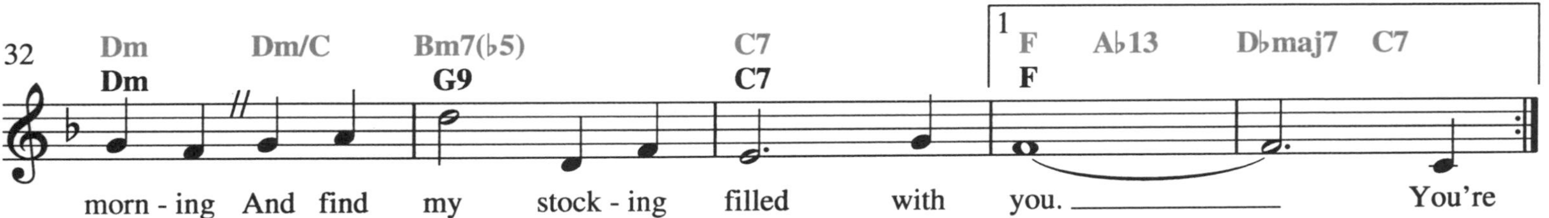

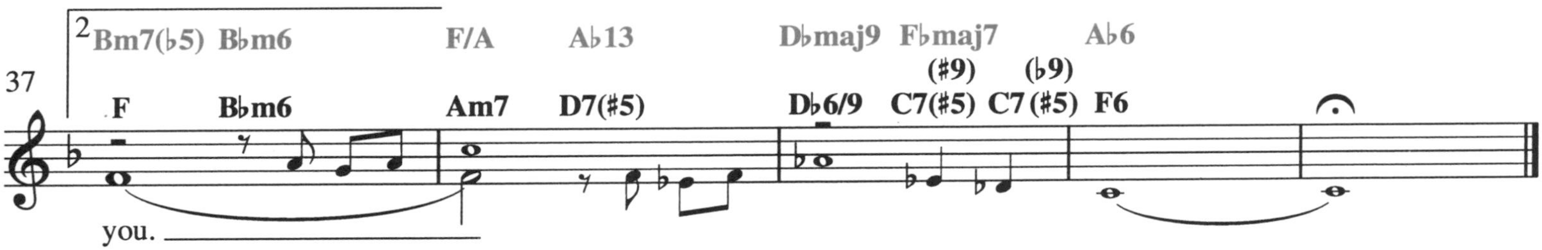

In bar 10, a B♭m6 is used in the substitute chord progression as it resolves better to the Am7(♭5) in bar 11 than the C7.

WE WISH YOU A MERRY CHRISTMAS